William Thomas Stead

**Hymns that have Helped**

William Thomas Stead
**Hymns that have Helped**
ISBN/EAN: 9783744779012

Printed in Europe, USA, Canada, Australia, Japan

Cover: Foto ©Thomas Meinert / pixelio.de

More available books at **www.hansebooks.com**

# Hymns that have Helped

Being a Collection of Hymns
which have been found most
useful to the Children of Men

Edited with the assistance
of numerous helpers by...

## W. T. Stead

✠

New York: Doubleday and
McClure Co. . . . . . 1898

*Copyright, 1897,*
BY DOUBLEDAY AND MCCLURE CO.

# PREFACE TO THE AMERICAN EDITION.

THE success which has attended the publication of the English edition of this little collection of "Hymns that have Helped," encourages the hope that it may be found equally acceptable to the American public.

The Service of Song is part of the Service of Man that is universal. It has hitherto been fortunate to escape the sectarian limitations of territorial and political divisions. According to an analysis made of the hymns contained in the most widely-used American hymn-books down to the year 1880, the average number of hymns of a purely American origin was not quite one in seven. There is probably no hymn-book in general use in any part of the British empire which does not count many American hymns among those which are most popular and helpful. Custom-houses may divide the producers and consumers of other manufactures. No Chinese wall of protective tariffs will ever prevent the two great English-speaking nations practising free trade in hymns. The English-speaking race has presumably no difficulty in recognising its unity when praising its Maker.

The principle upon which this collection has been compiled is more American than English. For the basic idea of the book is that of appealing directly to the experience of the individual; that of applying the test not of the standard of excellence of the literary expert, or of orthodoxy as defined by the authority of churches, but that of its helpfulness to men and women.

## 6   PREFACE TO AMERICAN EDITION.

I claim nothing for the collection beyond what its name implies. The hymns which it contains are hymns which have helped all sorts and conditions of men to do their work in this world and to face with composure or exultation the coming of the Messenger which summons them to the next. In its compilation I have naturally given the foremost place to those hymns which have helped those who have helped their fellows most. Some hymns are like jewelled chalices from which generation after generation has drunk of the water of life. Others are but as the rusty dipper from which the wayworn traveller cools his thirst. The workmanship of the vessel has weighed little compared with the authentic evidence that it was the means whereby the thirsty soul of man was able to drink and live.

In appealing to the American public I do not feel as if I were venturing upon ground that was more strange to me than that of my native land. For the English Nonconformist has always been more in fellowship with the churches of America than with the Anglican Church that is established and endowed in his own country. The men of the "Mayflower," who founded New England, and their descendants after them, have always been more of our kith and kin than the representatives of the church of Laud and the Stuarts. The children of the Puritans in the Old World and in the New form one family, in a much more real and vital sense than those who are outside the circle are able to realise. And within that circle there is no language of the household so familiar as sacred song.

It would be difficult to overestimate the extent to which the religious life of the English-speaking world has been quickened and gladdened by the Songs and Solos of Mr. Sankey. And before Mr. Sankey, the "American Sacred Songster" of Mr. Phillips had done much to enliven our Service of Song. To this day the American hymns and spiritual songs are more popular among our masses than any others. When mission

## PREFACE TO AMERICAN EDITION. 7

services are held, or a revival is under way, in the majority of cases the American hymns are used as a matter of course. This is not the case with the high Anglican services, but even there it would not be impossible to trace the influence of the inspiriting strains of the American Sacred Song.

When we know the favourite hymns of a man we have gained a glimpse into his inner life. When we know the hymns which have most helped the English of the Motherland, we gain more insight into the real trend of the aspirations and the deepest emotions of the nation than can be gained from the perusal of the entire British press. Hence, I hope it may be possible that in the United States this collection may be of some slight service in helping to a better understanding between the two nations. These hymns have been most helpful to us. What are the hymns which have been most helpful to you?

I want to publish as a sequel or supplement to this volume a second series of " Hymns that have Helped," based on the recorded experience of Americans. I do not know whether it may be possible to elicit an adequate response, but " nothing venture, nothing win."

The attempt to interrogate the foremost men and women in the States and Territories as to the hymns which have most helped them may possibly be less difficult where the Interviewer is indigenous than it is elsewhere. The experiment is well worth trying, but the experience gained in preparing the English edition suggested the expediency of slightly varying the form of interrogation.

I originally appealed to those who were willing to help in the work of compilation: first, for the personal experience of the individual addressed; second, for note or reference to record of instances where hymns had influenced those whose lives had greatly influenced the history of mankind; thirdly, for brief note of instances in which hymns had altered human lives, — even of the most obscure; and, fourthly, for reference to incidents where hymns had figured conspicuously in some notable episode in human history.

To these four I would add in making my appeal to the American public a fifth request; namely, that I should be furnished with the name of the living American whose life experience as to the helpful value of hymns my correspondent thinks would be most interesting and valuable to his countrymen.

May I ask all readers who are disposed to co-operate with me in preparing such an American sequel to the present volume to address their communications to me, care of the publishers of this volume, Doubleday & McClure Co., 141-155 East Twenty-fifth Street, New York, U. S. A.

W. T. STEAD.

# INTRODUCTION.

THERE are now nearly half a million hymns, nominally Christian, in the two hundred languages or dialects in which Christianity is preached.

The "Dictionary of Hymnology," compiled by the Rev. John Julian, M.A., contains over sixteen hundred closely-printed double-column pages, giving an account of some five thousand authors and translators of thirty thousand hymns,—not ten per cent of the immense mass.

There are said to be no fewer than 269 hymnals in the Church of England. But " Hymns Ancient and Modern " is rapidly ousting all others. In 1894 it was in use in over ten thousand churches. The "Hymnal Companion" had 1,478 supporters, run close by "Church Hymns" of the S. P. C. K. with 1,426, but only 379 used any other than these three collections. Of 1,058 London churches, " Hymns Ancient and Modern" were in use in 695. Of Methodist, Roman Catholic, Nonconformist, and Presbyterian hymnals there is no end. Yet, numerous as they are, the demand of the public for hymns continues unabated. How many hymn-books have been published this century no one can possibly say. But of " Hymns Ancient and Modern " no fewer than thirty-five millions have been circulated in the last thirty-five years, giving an average sale of close upon a million a year, or nearly three thousand per day, year in and year out, Sunday and week-day, ever since it was first published in 1860. It is impossible to estimate the number of hymn-books sold outside the Church of England at a less figure. We have, therefore, to face the amazing fact that of collections of sacred poetry the British public's normal regular consumption is two millions a year. It is thus possible that this collection, which is unique in its way, may have its share of popular support. It is at least of manageable dimensions. Most modern hymn-books suffer from corpulence. One thousand hymns seem to be regarded as the normal limit, a minimum which many compilers exceed.

In putting together the present list of about one hundred and fifty hymns, one feels somewhat like a captain of a cricket team selecting the first eleven for his county. Every one knows what resentment such a process necessarily creates among those who are relegated to the second eleven, and how all their friends deplore the blindness and injustice which led to their exclusion. Still, it cannot be helped; and although there are many hymns I should like to have seen in this selection, the limits are inexorable, and I have chosen my "first eleven" for better or for worse.

This Hymnal has been completed by the voluntary co-operation of a multitude of willing workers to whom I appealed, in the first place, for their own experience; in the second, for the well-authenticated record of how this or that hymn has helped those " whose lives sublime, shed undimmed splendour over unmeasured time ;" in the third place, for brief notes of instances in which hymns have altered human lives; and fourthly, for references to incidents such as that of the victor-psalm at Dunbar, where a hymn has figured conspicuously in some notable episode of human history.

This Hymnal has no claim to literary merit other than that which attaches to hymns which have a well-attested value as having been the channel through which mortal man has heard the voice of God, or which have enabled him to commune with his Maker. Some day I hope, if I may be spared, to edit a commentary on the Bible on similar principles.

Miss Hankey, the author of the very popular " Tell me the Old, Old Story," while writing with approval of the method of compiling this collection, adds a word of caution : —

## INTRODUCTION.   11

"Still waters run deep." We must not expect all who are helped by hymns to publish their special preferences and experiences, and among our own fellow-countrymen especially, every man's heart is his castle. Yet there are yearnings shared by all. To express and interpret these yearnings, to deepen and guide them, is the work of the hymn-writer.

The object of this collection, of course, is to ascertain what writers have succeeded best. It is a very difficult task, even when the compiler is assisted by correspondence from the uttermost ends of the earth.

Still, the task, though arduous, has been pleasant. Who can estimate the incalculable force for goodness and kindness and honest living that these hymns represent! Each of them is as seed-corn bearing harvests by which the nations live. That is true of all hymns, for in them dwells the real catholicity of the Christian Church. Well said Henry Ward Beecher:—

There is almost no heresy in the hymn-book. In hymns and psalms we have a universal ritual. It is the theology of the heart that unites men. Our very childhood is embalmed in sacred tunes and hymns. Our early lives and the lives of our parents hang in the atmosphere of sacred song. The art of singing together is one that is forever winding invisible threads about persons.

In hymns, as in iron-clads and many other inventions, France has led the way. Clement Marot was the first to popularise the Psalms as the Song Book of the people. "His version became the book of song in the castle as well as in the cottage, for recreation, and for at work; the lady at the hall, the weaver at the loom, the peasant at the plough, the first lesson taught to children, the last words whispered to or uttered by the dying man." I was reminded of the astonishing effect produced by the French innovation by the influence which the Salvation Army songs often exercise on a population which hears them for the first time. It was a sight to see and not to forget,— a string of cabmen at a north-country station sitting on a fence, singing the hymns of the Salvation Army in the intervals between the trains.

The same thing was observed in Germany and in Scotland. Luther's doctrine would have fallen comparatively flat had not his psalms and hymns given wings to his teaching. They were carried all over the country by wandering students and pedlers, and became so popular that they even found their way into the Roman Catholic Church, so that a Romanist declared: "The whole people is singing itself into the Lutheran doctrine."

And no wonder; for Luther was one of the first to mark the great truth that the tune is more important than the words. With him the tune was first, the words second. Luther fashioned the words to the tune. "The rhythm of the song was always in his ear as he worked on it; he carefully fitted the syllables to the notes. In certain places it is seen that he did violence to the language to fit it to the exigencies of the music." But the German reformer had a good notion of what a tune should be. He said:—

> The words of hymns should have a swing and a good strong metre, so that the congregation might catch up the tune to join in with it. Let us bid good-bye to the music of Gregory, and take the common songs of our own people, as they sing them at harvests, at village festivals, at weddings, and at funerals, for use in our churches. Man can as well praise God in one tune as the other, and it is a pity that such pretty songs as these should be kept any longer from the service of their Maker.

Mr. Reginald Brett went too far when he declared that the music and congregational singing were the causes of emotion, and not the words of any hymn; but there is no doubt that Mr. Balfour was right when he said:—

> One of the great merits of hymns lies in the associations which attach to them, from which it follows that they cannot really be considered apart from the tunes to which they are habitually set. In my opinion, the editor of a hymn-book who

deliberately divorces old words from their accustomed setting is an iconoclast of the worst order.

I hope that in affixing as far as possible the old familiar tunes to this collection, I may escape the major excommunication.

It is a fashion in some quarters to sneer at the poetical value of hymns. A glance, however, through the pages of this collection, will suffice to show that, while some hymns may fall far below the standard of first-class poetry, many, if not the majority, will fairly rank with the best verse that our race has produced. Modern hymnologists are no longer of the opinion of the worthy men who compiled a hymn-book for one of the straiter sects of orthodox dissenters, in which it is gravely set forth that "poetry itself is objectionable as bearing the spirit and imagination of man." On this I am glad to have Mrs. Meynell's mature and dispassionate judgment against the disparaging observations of Mr. William Morris and Mr. Coventry Patmore. Mrs. Meynell says:—

Hymns have, and doubtless always will have, a power over men's minds; and I don't wonder at it, for I think — against the usual literary opinion — that many popular hymns are very beautiful, and that their authors made literature without knowing it. Personally I have none of those early associations with hymns. I never heard any in my childhood. Consequently, I think I have been touched by the real beauty of hymns, and not by the mere accident of association.

There only remains one word to say as to the extremely broad view which I have taken of my duties as an editor. Never before in any popular hymnal have hymns to the Virgin jostled the Confession of the Jewish faith, revolutionary songs elbowed the ancient anthems of the Church, while psalms and hymns and spiritual songs of all countries and of all creeds and of none stand side by side on an equal footing, each exhibiting as its sole credential that it has helped the human heart to love, to dare, and to aspire, and strengthened man to bear his part worthily in the warfare of life. It is well when we introduce the million to the study of comparative religion that the Religions should be on their best behaviour. All religions show their best manners in sacred song. But until this little book chanced to fall into the hands of its readers, how many of them were utterly oblivious of the treasures of beauty, of wisdom, and of love that were to be found outside the cover of the hymn-book of their own church? Here at least Roman, Greek, Lutheran, Calvinist, Methodist, Unitarian, and Jew are recognisable only by the common accents of a common faith in the One Father in Whose family all we are brethren.

# PREFACE.

THE songs of the English-speaking people are for the most part hymns. For the immense majority of our people to-day the only minstrelsy is that of the hymn-book. And this is as true of our race beyond the sea as it is of our race at home.

Of the making of collections of hymns there is no end. But so far as I have been able to discover, no collection of hymns has ever been made based upon the principle of including in it only those hymns which have been most helpful to the men and women who have most influenced their fellow-men. Yet surely those hymns which have most helped the greatest and best of our race are those which bear, as it were, the hall-mark of Heaven.

The root idea of this Hymnal is to select the hymns, not by the fine or finical ear of the critic in the study, or even by the exalted judgment of the recluse in the cloister, but by the recorded experience of mankind. Here and thus did this hymn help me : that is the best of all possible arguments in favour of believing that it will prove helpful under similar circumstances to similar characters. The hymn may be doggerel poetry, it may contain heretical theology, its grammar may be faulty and its metaphors atrocious, but if that hymn proved itself a staff and a stay to some heroic soul in the darkest hours of his life's pilgrimage, then that hymn has won its right to a place among the sacred songs through which God has spoken to the soul of man.

Who is there among the men and women of this generation who has not, at some time or other, experienced the strange and subtle influence of sacred song? Hymns have rung in the ears of some of us while still wandering idly in the streets of the City of Destruction, stern and shrill as the bugle-blast that rouses the sleeping camp to prepare for the onslaught of the foe. Their melody has haunted the ear amid the murmur of the mart and the roar of the street. In the storm and stress of life's battle the echo of their sweet refrain has renewed our strength and dispelled our fears. They have been, as it were, the voices of the angels of God, and when we have heard them we could hear no other sound, neither the growling of the lions in the path nor the curses and threatenings of the fiends from the pit. Around the hymn and the hymn tune how many associations gather from the earliest days, when, as infants, we were hushed to sleep on our mother's lap by their monotonous chant! At this moment, on the slope of the Rockies, or in the sweltering jungles of India, in crowded Australian city, or secluded English hamlet, the sound of some simple hymn tune will, as by mere magic spell, call from the silent grave the shadowy forms of the unforgotten dead, and transport the listener, involuntarily, over land and sea, to the scene of his childhood's years, to the village school, to the parish church. In our pilgrimage through life we discover the hymns which help. We come out of trials and temptations with hymns clinging to our memory like burrs. Some of us could almost use the hymn-book as the key to our autobiography. Hymns, like angels and other ministers of grace, often help us and disappear into the void. It is not often that the hymn of our youth is the hymn of our old age. Experience of life is the natural selector of the truly human hymnal.

There is a curious and not a very creditable shrinking on the part of many to testify as to their experience in the deeper matters of the soul. It is an inverted egotism, — selfishness masquerading in disguise of reluctance to speak of self. Wanderers across the wilderness of Life ought not to be chary of telling their fellow-travellers where they found the green oasis, the healing spring, or the shadow of a great rock in a desert land.

# PREFACE.

It is not regarded as egotism when the passing steamer signals across the Atlantic wave news of her escape from perils of iceberg or fog, or welcome news of good cheer. Yet individuals shrink into themselves, repressing rigorously the fraternal instinct which bids them communicate the fruits of their experience to their fellows. Therein they deprive themselves of a share in the communion of saints, and refuse to partake with their brother of the sacramental cup of human sympathy, or to break the sacred bread of the deeper experiences.

"Hymns that have Helped Me." What hymns have helped you? And if they have helped you, how can you better repay the debt you owe to your helper than by setting them forth, stamped with the tribute of your gratitude, to help other mortals in like straits to yourself? All of us have our moments when we are near to the mood of the hero and the saint, and it is something to know what hymns help most to take us there, and keep us at that higher pitch.

Such in substance was my appeal. I sent it out in broadcast, and received many widely varying responses. Lord Rosebery, for instance, declined "confession in general" to the public on the subject. The Archbishop of Canterbury referred me to a hymnal which he himself had compiled many years ago. The Prince of Wales indicated his preference for Mrs. Adams' well-known hymn. The Dean of St. Paul's disapproved of the principle of the hymn-book, and wrote as follows: —

I imagine that hymns are one of the best instruments for implanting religious ideas in the minds of children, and as I cannot think of any religion that can have the desired influence from which the essential doctrines of Christianity are excluded, I must decline to accept your courteous invitation to take part in compiling an unsectarian hymn book.

As if the "essential doctrines" must be excluded because the Hymnal is unsectarian!

Mr. Grant Allen replied: —

I do not remember that any hymn, or, for the matter of that, any text of scripture, maxim, or line of poetry, was ever of the least use to me. There are poems which I love, such as Shelley's "Skylark;" but I cannot honestly say they ever "helped" me. I never needed help, other than physical or monetary. My own philosophy has always amply sufficed me.

It is no doubt difficult to obtain a frank and full statement as to the " Hymns that have Helped " people, owing to the fact that all such confessions must be more or less autobiographical, and deal with the hidden matters of inner spiritual life. The Bishop of Winchester says:—

I agree with you in thinking that a compilation made in the manner and on the lines proposed will have a special interest, and, subject to the limitations I refer to in this note, I heartily wish you success in your endeavour; but I am not quite at one with you in regarding it to be the duty of all who could do so to tell you for publication not merely what hymns they have found helpful, but how, and where, and when the help has been given. To do this with any approach to completeness would require not an autobiography only, but an autobiography respecting the sins, the sorrows, the temptations, and the blessings of the inner life of each one of us. There may be a few men who can make such thoughts and memory public without harm to themselves or others, but the number of such is small, and I am not of them.

Mrs. Humphry Ward goes further than the Bishop, and maintains that she cannot help saying that the question she is asked seems to her to be just that one which should not be answered, if one sets any value upon religious feeling and religious life. This is rather a hard saying, coming as it does from the author of "Robert Elsmere," which is a more or less successful attempt to unveil the hidden movements of religious thought and religious life in the soul of her hero before the eyes of the million.

Dr. Rigg, the well-known Wesleyan Methodist minister, noted with a certain grim satisfaction the Methodist note in my appeal for experiences, and made me out a list of hymns which he found peculiarly helpful as customary and companion-aids in times of spiritual need. He said:—

In my list of hymns I do not include such hymns or religious poems as may have deeply touched my sympathy and even expressed my feelings, but yet at the same time have not been the means of lifting me above myself into the region of faith or hope, or in any way of strengthening me against my moods of despondency or weakness.

One eminent philosopher excused himself from contributing on grounds characteristically stated in the following letter:—

DEAR SIR,—I fear I shall be unable to aid you in the undertaking described in your letter of the 11th. My own experience furnishes no examples of the kind you wish. If parents had more sense than is commonly found among them, they would never dream of setting their children to learn hymns as tasks. With me the effect was not to generate any liking for this or that hymn, but to generate a dislike for hymns at large. The process of learning was a penalty, and the feeling associated with that penalty became a feeling associated with hymns in general. Hence it results that I cannot name any "hymn that has helped me." — Faithfully yours, HERBERT SPENCER.

On the other hand, Mr. Mark Whitwell, the well-known citizen and philanthropist of Bristol, sends me a list of twenty-three hymns, all of which he committed to memory before he was four years of age. He writes:—

I really enjoyed learning them; it was a real pleasure to me, partly because it gave my father so much pleasure to hear me repeat them.

For my own part, I will gladly take my turn with the rest in testifying, conscious though I am that the hymn which helped me most can lay no claim to pre-eminent merit as poetry. It is Newton's hymn, which begins, " Begone, unbelief." I can remember my mother singing it when I was a tiny boy, barely able to see over the book-ledge in the minister's pew; and to this day, whenever I am in doleful dumps, and the stars in their courses appear to be fighting against me, that one doggerel verse comes back clear as a blackbird's note through the morning mist:—

> His love in time past
> Forbids me to think
> He'll leave me at last
> In trouble to sink.
>
> Each sweet Ebenezer
> I have in review
> Confirms his good pleasure
> To help me quite through.

The rhyme is bad enough, no doubt; the logic may or may not be rational; but the verse as it is, with all its shortcomings, has been as a life-buoy, keeping my head above the waves when the sea raged and was tempestuous, and when all else failed. What that verse has been to me, other verses have been to other men and other women. And what I have tried to do in this "Penny Hymnal" is to collate from the multitudinous record of diversified human experience the hymns which have helped most, in order to present them with some record of how, and where, and when, and whom they have helped, as a compendious collection for the use of every one.

I have to express my indebtedness to many friends and helpers of all sorts and conditions of men and women who have communicated with me on the subject of "Hymns that have Helped." The books which have been most helpful are Julian's monumental "Dictionary of Hymns," Horder's "Hymn-Lover," Duffield's "English Hymns," Marson's "Psalms at Work," Dr. Ker's "The Psalms in History and Biography," and Stevenson's "Notes on the Methodist Hymn Book."

I have also to acknowledge my indebtedness to the following authors or owners of copyright hymns for permission kindly given to use them in this collection:

# PREFACE. 21

To the Rev. S. Baring-Gould for "Onward, Christian Soldiers;" to the representatives of the late Dean Alford for the use of "Forward be our Watchword;" to the Society for Promoting Christian Knowledge for the use of the Rev. J. E. Bode's hymn, "O Jesu, I have promised," and the Rev. J. E. Ellerton's "Now the labourer's task is o'er;" to Mrs. Blackie for Prof. Blackie's hymn, "Angels holy, high and lowly;" to the Right Rev. Bishop of Exeter, Dr. Bickersteth, for his hymn, "Peace, perfect peace;" to the Rev. Father Neville for permission to use Cardinal Newman's hymn, "Lead, kindly Light;" to Dr. Matheson for his hymn, "O Love that will not let me go;" to Canon Twells for "At Even, ere the Sun was set;" to Messrs. James Nisbet and Co. for kindly consenting to the use of several of the late Dr. Bonar's hymns, as well as a hymn by Miss Havergal; to Mr. Wm. Isbister for the late Dr. Macleod's hymn, "Courage, Brother, do not stumble;" to Mrs. Linnæus Banks, for a poem by her late husband; to Messrs. Morgan and Scott for seven hymns from "Sacred Songs and Solos;" to Messrs. Burns and Oates for certain of the Latin translations given in the earlier part of this collection; and finally to Mr. Herbert Booth, for his hymn, "Blessed Lord, in Thee is Refuge."

I hope I may be pardoned if, in spite of all efforts to discover the owners of copyright, I have unwittingly infringed any copyright, or failed to acknowledge my indebtedness for the use of these hymns.

# Hymns that Have Helped

## I. — Praise.

### 1 — THE TE DEUM.

THE Te Deum properly stands first in any collection of Hymns that Helped. For it is the most catholic of hymns, one of the oldest and one of the most universally used by the entire Western Church. What God Save the Queen has been for a century or more to modern England, the Te Deum has been to Christendom, divided and undivided, for more than a thousand years. It was chanted at the baptism of Clovis, and it was sung at the Jubilee of Queen Victoria. It was in regular use as a Sunday morning hymn in the beginning of the sixth century, and it was chanted the other day at the coronation of Nicholas II. at Moscow. No other hymn of praise has been by such universal consent set apart as the supreme expression of the overflowing gratitude of the human heart. According to the precise ritual of the Roman Church, it must be sung at the three supreme acts of solemn worship, — the Consecration of a Bishop, the Coronation of a King, and the Consecration of a Virgin. To these have been added others, — the Election of a Pope, the Canonization of a Saint, the publication of a Treaty of Peace, or the conclusion of a Treaty of Alliance in favour of the Church. It has from of old figured in our coronation service, and whenever the national heart is stirred by some great deliverance by hard-won victory on sea or land, or by the recovery of some beloved sovereign, or any other event which causes the common universal heart to throb, there and then is the Te Deum sung. After the fifth Harry had won the battle of Agincourt, he cried:—

> "Do we all holy rites, Let there be sung
> Non Nobis, and Te Deum."

As it was sung after Agincourt, so it was sung after Waterloo, and will be sung after other victories yet unfought by generations yet unborn. Whenever the hearts of the men and women of the West throb high with emotions of gratitude too deep for non-rhythmic words, it is to the Te Deum that they turn for help; there alone have they for generation after generation found adequate expression. Of versions of the Te Deum there are as many as there are languages spoken by man. In this collection, which is popular and not critical, I follow, for the Latin, the text in the Roman Catholic Service Book, and, for the English, the version of the Book of Common Prayer.

WE praise Thee, O God: we acknowledge Thee to be the Lord.

All the earth doth worship Thee, the Father everlasting.

To Thee all angels cry aloud: the heavens and all the powers therein.

To Thee Cherubin and Seraphin continually do cry,

Holy, holy, holy, Lord God of Sabaoth;

Heaven and earth are full of the majesty of Thy glory.

The glorious company of the Apostles praise Thee.

The goodly fellowship of the Prophets praise Thee.

The noble army of Martyrs praise Thee.

The holy Church throughout all the world doth acknowledge Thee;
The Father of an Infinite Majesty;
Thine honourable, true, and only Son;
Also the Holy Ghost, the Comforter.
Thou art the King of Glory, O Christ.
Thou art the everlasting Son of the Father.
When thou tookest upon Thee to deliver man, Thou didst not abhor the Virgin's womb.
When Thou hadst overcome the sharpness of death, Thou didst open the kingdom of heaven to all believers.
Thou sittest at the right hand of God, in the glory of the Father.
We believe that Thou shalt come to be our Judge.
We therefore pray Thee, help Thy servants whom Thou hast redeemed with Thy precious blood.
Make them to be numbered with Thy saints in glory everlasting.
O Lord, save Thy people, and bless Thine heritage.
Govern them, and lift them up for ever.
Day by day we magnify Thee;
And we worship Thy name ever world without end.
Vouchsafe, O Lord, to keep us this day without sin.
O Lord, have mercy upon us, have mercy upon us.
O Lord, let Thy mercy lighten upon us, as our trust is in Thee.
O Lord, in Thee have I trusted, let me never be confounded.

TE Deum laudamus: te Dominum confitemur.
  Te æternum Patrem: omnis terra veneratur.
Tibi omnes Angeli: tibi coeli, et universæ potestates.
Tibi Cherubim et Seraphim; incessabili voce proclamant,
Sanctus, Sanctus, Sanctus: Dominus Deus Sabaoth;
Pleni sunt coeli et terra: majestatis gloriæ tuæ.
Te gloriosus: Apostolorum chorus.
Te Prophetarum: laudabilis numerus.
Te Martyrum candidatus: laudat exercitus.
Te per orbem terrarum: sancta confitetur Ecclesia;
Patrem: immensæ majestatis;
Venerandum tuum verum: et unicum Filium.
Sanctum quoque: Paraclitum Spiritum.
Tu Rex gloriæ: Christe.
Tu Patris: sempiternus es Filius.
Tu ad liberandum suscepturus hominem: non horruisti Virginis uterum.
Tu devicto mortis aculeo: aperuisti credentibus regna coelorum.
Tu ad dexteram Dei sedes: in gloria Patris.
Judex crederis: esse venturus.
Te ergo quæsumus, tuis famulis subveni: quos pretioso sanguine redemisti.
Æterna fac cum Sanctis tuis: in gloria numerari.
Salvum fac populum tuum, Domine: et benedic hæreditati tuæ.
Et rege eos: et extolle illos, usque in æternum.
Per singulos dies: benedicimus te.
Et laudamus nomen tuum in sæculum: et in sæculum sæculi
Dignare, Domine, die isto: sine peccatis nos custodire.

Miserere nostri, Domine: miserere nostri.

Fiat misericordia tua, Domine, supernos: quemadmodum speravimus in te.

In te, Domine, speravi: non confundar in æternum.

Very shortly before her decease, Mrs. Charles, the author of the "Schönberg-Cotta Family," "Songs, Old and New," and "The Voice of Christian Life and Song," wrote me, in reply to my inquiry as to which hymns had helped her, saying: "The Te Deum, with its glorious objectiveness, its tender humility, and its note of hope, has, perhaps, helped me and inspired me through life more than any other hymn."

As some Nonconformists may possibly object to the inclusion of such pieces as the Te Deum and the Magnificat in a collection of hymns, I may quote a line from the Rev. Hugh Price Hughes' letter to me, in which he says: "I hope that in any book you publish you will include the *Te Deum*, in many respects the most majestic as well as the most venerable hymn of the Christian Church."

There is, of course, another side to this. If the Te Deum has been used to express the gratitude of man for crowning mercies, it has often been used as a kind of Christian war-whoop over fallen foes. If our forefathers sang it with full hearts when England was delivered from the fell menace of the Armada, it was also chanted at Rome in honour of the massacre of St. Bartholomew. If, as an ancient heathen poet declared, —

> " Unholy is the sound
> Of loud thanksgiving over slaughtered men,"

impious indeed must have been the exultant strains that have gone up on high over the hecatombs of the battlefield. But this prostitution of the great Christian hymn in the service of un-Christian statecraft and sceptred murder has probably never been better exposed than by Kinglake in his memorable description of the

Te Deum in Notre Dame, "that historic pile which stands mocking the lapse of ages and the strange checkered destiny of France." Napoleon, fresh from the massacre of the Boulevards, his lips reeking with perjury, and his hands all red with blood, came "into the presence of God."

"When the Church perceived that the swearer of the oath and all his associates were ready, she began her service. Having robes whereon all down the back there was embroidered the figure of a cross, and being, it would seem, without fear, the bishops and priests went up to the high altar and scattered rich incense, and knelt and rose, and knelt and rose again. Then, in the hearing of thousands, there pealed through the aisles that hymn of praise which purports to waft into heaven the thanksgivings of a whole people for some new and signal mercy vouchsafed to them by Almighty God. It was because of what had been done to France within the last thirty days that the hosannas arose in Notre Dame. Moreover, the priests lifted their voices and cried aloud, chanting and saying to the Most High, 'Domine, salvum fac Ludovicum Napoleonem,'— O Lord! save Louis Napoleon.

"What is good, and what is evil? and who is it that deserves the prayers of a nation? If any man, being scrupulous and devout, was moved by the events of December to ask these questions of his Church, he was answered that day in the Cathedral of Our Lady in Paris."[1]

## 2 — THE ENGLISH TE DEUM.

If the Te Deum be the Hymn of Praise set apart by the Universal Church as the supreme expression of gratitude and adoration, the hymn which serves the same purpose in English congregations is "All Hail the Power of Jesu's Name." It is one of the ten hymns most used in English-speaking lands. It was written

[1] History of Crimean War, vol. i. p. 335.

near the close of last century by E. Perronet, a minister of Lady Huntingdon's Connection, but was subsequently much revised by Dr. Rippon and others. The form most commonly used is as follows:—

ALL hail the power of Jesu's name!
   Let angels prostrate fall;
Bring forth the royal diadem,
   And crown Him Lord of all.

Let high-born seraphs tune the lyre,
   And, as they tune it, fall
Before His face who tunes their choir,
   And crown Him Lord of all.

Crown Him, ye martyrs of your God,
   Who from his altar call;
Extol the stem from Jesse's rod,
   And crown Him Lord of all.

Ye seed of Israel's chosen race,
   Ye ransomed from the Fall,
Hail Him who saves you by His grace,
   And crown Him Lord of all.

Sinners! whose love can ne'er forget
   The wormwood and the gall,
Go, spread your trophies at His feet,
   And crown Him Lord of all.

Let every kindred, every tribe,
   On this terrestrial ball,
To Him all majesty ascribe,
   And crown Him Lord of all.

O that with yonder sacred throng
   We at His feet may fall,
Join in the everlasting song,
   And crown Him Lord of all!

                  TUNE—"MILES LANE."

## 3—THE SCOTCH TE DEUM.

THE Scotch Church for nearly three hundred years refused to have anything to do with human hymns, papistical Te Deums, and the like. But in the metrical version of the Hundredth Psalm, the men of North Britain found a practical substitute which stood them in good stead as a vehicle for the expression of their usually repressed emotions. It was written by W. Kethe in 1560-61, to fit the tune in the Genevan Psalter now known as the Old Hundredth.

It is one of the few Psalms to which Shakespeare makes reference in his plays.

ALL people that on earth do dwell,
    Sing to the Lord with cheerful voice:
Him serve with mirth, His praise forth tell;
    Come ye before Him and rejoice.

Know ye, the Lord is God indeed;
    Without our aid He did us make;
We are His flock, He doth us feed;
    And for His sheep He doth us take.

Oh enter then His gates with praise,
    Approach with joy His courts unto;
Praise, laud, and bless His name always,
    For it is seemly so to do.

For why? the Lord our God is good,
    His mercy is for ever sure;
His truth at all times firmly stood,
    And shall from age to age endure.

TUNE— "OLD HUNDREDTH."

Longfellow refers to the New England settlers

"Singing the Hundredth Psalm, that grand old Puritan anthem."

The Rev. James Campbell, of Dublin, says: "The magnificent version of the Hundredth, set to Luther's majestic tune, has wedded Lutherans and Calvinists to eternity, and girdled the earth with sweet and stately praise."

## 4—THE GERMAN TE DEUM.

RINKART'S hymn, "Nun Danket alle Gott," comes second only to Luther's "Ein' feste Burg." The latter is a hymn of combat and of resolution to battle to the end, the former an outburst of gratitude. It is a paraphrase of two verses of Ecclesiasticus, and in verse 3 of one verse of the Gloria Patri. It has been used since 1648 as the German Te Deum at all national festivals of war and of peace. It was sung by the army of Frederick the Great after the Prussians had won the Battle of Leuthen, and it was constantly sung in the last Franco-Prussian War. It was also sung at the ceremony that marked the completion of Cologne Cathedral and at the laying of the foundation-stone of the new Reichstag.

Mendelssohn introduces "Nun Danket" into his "Hymn of Praise." The following translation is by Catherine Winkworth:—

NOW thank we all our God,
    With heart, and hands, and voices,
Who wondrous things hath done,
    In Whom His world rejoices;
    Who from our mothers' arms
      Hath blessed us on our way
    With countless gifts of love,
    And still is ours to-day.

O may this bounteous God
Through all our life be near us,
    With ever joyful hearts
And blessèd peace to cheer us;

And keep us in his grace,
　　And guide us when perplex'd,
　And free us from all ills
　　In this world and the next.

　All praise and thanks to God
The Father now be given,
　　The Son, and Him who reigns
With them in highest Heaven,
　The One eternal God,
　　Whom earth and Heav'n adore,
　For thus it was, is now,
　　And shall be evermore.　Amen.

　　TUNE — "WITTEMBURG," SOMETIMES CALLED "NUN DANKET."

## 5 — THE DOXOLOGY.

PROBABLY no other verse is so often sung by Christians of all denominations as this brief outburst of praise and gratitude; and yet the glad devotion expressed in any of the numerous adaptations never fails to kindle an audience. Originally written as the closing stanzas of "Awake my soul, and with the sun," the author, Bishop Ken (1637–1711), derived so much benefit from the use of it in his morning devotions that he added it to his now equally famous evening hymn, "Glory to Thee, my God, this night." It was the habit of this saintly sufferer to accompany his ever cheerful voice with the lute which penetrated beyond his prison walls; and the oft-repeated song of praise, which was soon taken up by his religious sympathisers listening without, has gone on singing itself into the hearts of Christians until the fragment has very nearly approached the hymn universal.

During revivals it is sometimes the custom to sing it after every conversion. Once at Sheffield, England, under Billy Dawson, they sang it thirty-five times in one evening. It is frequently the last articulate sound that is heard from the lips of the dying, and it is not less frequently the expression of intense gratitude of the living in the moments when life throbs and swells most exultantly in the breast.

PRAISE God from Whom all blessings flow!
Praise Him, all creatures here below!
Praise Him above, ye heavenly host!
Praise Father, Son, and Holy Ghost!

## 6—HEBER'S TRINITY-SUNDAY HYMN.

THE Head Master of Harrow, after mentioning the three hymns which had helped him most, said: "I put them in what may be called an order of merit as follows:—1. 'Hark, my soul, it is the Lord.' 2. 'O God, our help in ages past.' 3. 'Rock of Ages, cleft for me.' Perhaps you will let me add that Bishop Heber's Trinity-Sunday Hymn, 'Holy, holy, holy, Lord God Almighty,' though it cannot be said to have given me most help, yet is in my judgment the finest hymn ever written, considering the abstract difficult nature of its theme, its perfect spirituality, and the devotion and purity of its language. The late Poet Laureate once told me he thought so too."

HOLY, holy, holy, Lord God Almighty!
Early in the morning our song shall rise to Thee;
Holy, holy, holy, merciful and mighty!
God in Three Persons, blessèd Trinity!

Holy, holy, holy! all the saints adore Thee,
Casting down their golden crowns around the glassy sea,
Cherubim and Seraphim falling down before Thee,
Which wert, and art, and evermore shalt be.

Holy, holy, holy! though the darkness hide Thee,
  Though the eye of sinful man Thy glory may
    not see,
Only Thou art holy, there is none beside Thee,
  Perfect in power, in love, and purity.

Holy, holy, holy, Lord God Almighty!
  All Thy works shall praise Thy name in earth
    and sky and sea;
Holy, holy, holy, merciful and mighty!
  God in Three Persons, blessèd Trinity.

TUNE — "NICÆA."

## 7—MILTON'S PSALM OF PRAISE
### (17th Century).

MILTON, our greatest poet save one, wrote only one hymn that has been found to help men — as a hymn. It is a paraphrase of Psalm cxxxvi. written when he was a boy of fifteen at St. Paul's School, and its length — twenty-four stanzas — precludes its general use. Those verses found most helpful by general usage are the following: —

LET us, with a gladsome mind,
  Praise the Lord, for He is kind:
For His mercies aye endure,
Ever faithful, ever sure.

Let us sound His name abroad,
For of gods He is the God:
For His mercies aye endure,
Ever faithful, ever sure.

He, with all commanding might,
Filled the new-made world with light:
For His mercies aye endure,
Ever faithful, ever sure.

He the golden-tressed sun
Caused all day his course to run:
For His mercies aye endure,
Ever faithful, ever sure.

All things living He doth feed:
His full hand supplies their need:
For His mercies aye endure,
Ever faithful, ever sure.

He His chosen race did bless,
In the wasteful wilderness:
For His mercies aye endure,
Ever faithful, ever sure.

He hath, with a piteous eye,
Looked upon our misery:
For His mercies aye endure,
Ever faithful, ever sure.

Let us, then, with gladsome mind,
Praise the Lord, for He is kind:
For His mercies aye endure,
Ever faithful, ever sure.

TUNE— "INNOCENTS."

## 8—ADDISON'S "GRATITUDE" (18th Century).

"I PERCEIVE," said Mr. Andrew Lang recently, "that either the best English poets have not written hymns, or that their hymns are unpopular with readers of the *Sunday at Home.*" Yet Milton was represented, and Cowper and Keble and Newman. Addison can hardly claim to be one of the best English poets, although he is one of the most famous essayists; but his contributions to Hymns that have Helped are by no means unimportant. Of these one of the most generally used is his poem originally published in the *Spectator* at the close of an essay on gratitude.[1]

WHEN all Thy mercies, O my God,
    My rising soul surveys,
Transported with the view, I 'm lost
    In wonder, love, and praise.

Oh how shall words with equal warmth
    The gratitude declare,
That glows within my thankful heart?
    But Thou canst read it there.

Thy providence my life sustained,
    And all my wants redressed,
When in the silent womb I lay,
    And hung upon the breast.

Unnumbered comforts on my soul
    Thy tender care bestowed,
Before my infant heart conceived
    From whom those comforts flowed.

When in the slippery paths of youth
    With heedless steps I ran,
Thine arm, unseen, conveyed me safe,
    And led me up to man.

[1] On the appearance of the first edition of this work a correspondent wrote calling my attention to the fact that in the *Athenæum* of July 10, 1880, and in the *Phonetic Journal* of March 12, 1887, it was conclusively proved that the author of this hymn was not Addison, but one Richard Richmond, rector of Walton-on-the-Hill, Lancashire, 1690–1720. On the other hand, Mr. T. M. Healy, M. P., wrote saying that the late Sir Isaac Pitman, in an interesting inquiry as to the authorship of this hymn and the other attributed to Addison on page 232. claimed both as the work of Andrew Marvel, the "incorruptible Commoner."

When worn with sickness, oft hast Thou
  With health renewed my face;
And, when in sins and sorrows sunk,
  Revived my soul with grace.

Ten thousand thousand precious gifts
  My daily thanks employ;
Nor is the least a cheerful heart,
  That tastes those gifts with joy.

Through every period of my life
  Thy goodness I 'll pursue;
And, after death, in distant worlds,
  The glorious theme renew.

Through all eternity to Thee
  A joyful song I 'll raise:
But Oh! eternity's too short
  To utter all Thy praise.

TUNE — "ST. PETER'S."

## 9 — PROFESSOR BLACKIE'S CHANT OF PRAISE (19th Century).

THE late Professor Blackie wrote much that is forgotten, but his Chant of Praise will live. It was sent me by one who had felt the glory and inspiration of its nature-worship cheer him like a sea-breeze. It is the nineteenth-century version of the sentiment which Milton expressed in the seventeenth and Addison in the eighteenth, each in the mode of his day and generation.

ANGELS holy,
  High and lowly,
Sing the praises of the Lord!
Earth and sky, all living nature,
Man, the stamp of thy Creator,
  Praise ye, praise ye, God the Lord!

> Sun and moon bright,
> Night and moonlight,
> Starry temples azure-floored;
> Cloud and rain, and wild winds' madness,
> Sons of God that shout for gladness,
> Praise ye, praise ye, God the Lord!
>
> Ocean hoary,
> Tell His glory,
> Cliffs, where tumbling seas have roared!
> Pulse of waters, blithely beating,
> Wave advancing, wave retreating,
> Praise ye, praise ye, God the Lord!
>
> Rock and high land,
> Wood and island,
> Crag, where eagle's pride hath soared;
> Mighty mountains, purple-breasted,
> Peaks cloud-cleaving, snowy-crested,
> Praise ye, praise ye, God the Lord!
>
> Rolling river,
> Praise Him ever,
> From the mountain's deep vein poured;
> Silver fountain, clearly gushing,
> Troubled torrent, madly rushing,
> Praise ye, praise ye, God the Lord!
>
> Bond and free man,
> Land and seaman,
> Earth, with peoples widely stored,
> Wanderer lone o'er prairies ample,
> Full-voiced choir, in costly temple,
> Praise ye, praise ye, God the Lord!
>
> Praise Him ever,
> Bounteous Giver;
> Praise Him, Father, Friend, and Lord!

HYMNS THAT HAVE HELPED. 39

> Each glad soul its free course winging,
> Each glad voice its free song singing,
>   Praise the great and mighty Lord!

The Rev. Richard A. Armstrong, of Liverpool, says: "To my mind this is one of the noblest bits of nature-painting in literature. I always give it out to my people after holiday-making in Norway or Scotland, and the

> Mighty mountains, purple-breasted,
> Peaks cloud-cleaving, snowy-crested,

rise up in vision before us again in glory. It is paganism, perhaps, but it is paganism through which thrills the presence of the God of Christ."

This poem of Blackie is at least not open to the objection taken by Charles Kingsley to many hymns. Kingsley says: "How often is the tone in which hymns speak of the natural world one of dissatisfaction, distrust, almost contempt. 'Change and decay in all around I see,' is their keynote rather than 'O all ye works of the Lord, bless ye the Lord, praise Him, and magnify Him for ever.'"

An anonymous writer, in whose sentiments Kingsley would have rejoiced, wrote a poem entitled "The Voice of Health," in illustration of the words, "The living he shall praise Thee." There are six stanzas, one of which will suffice to give the keynote:—

> 'Tis when youth's fervour fills the veins,
>   And new-born hopes rejoice the heart,
> And health within and round us reigns,
>   We best believe Thee as Thou art.

## II.—National Hymns.

### 10—GOD SAVE THE QUEEN.

GOD save our gracious Queen,
  Long live our noble Queen;
God save the Queen!

Send her victorious,
Happy and glorious,
Long to reign over us,
  God save the Queen!

O Lord our God, arise,
Scatter her enemies,
  And make them fall.
Confound their politics!
Frustrate their knavish tricks;
On her our hopes we fix!
  God save us all!

Thy choicest gifts in store,
On her be pleased to pour;
  Long may she reign!
May she defend our laws,
And ever give us cause
To sing with heart and voice,
  God save the Queen!

     TUNE — "THE NATIONAL ANTHEM."

It is one of the ironies of history that the first trace that can be discovered of the singing of the English National Anthem, imploring Divine help for the reigning monarch, was an occasion when its petition was most conspicuously refused. In 1688, when William of Orange was busy with his preparations in aid of the conspiracy against the Stuart dynasty, a Latin chorus was sung in the private chapel of James II., which appears to have been the original of the famous anthem. We can well imagine the fervour with which James II. and his devout satellites joined in the petition thus voiced by the choir:—

| O Deus Optime! | Exurgat Dominus; |
| Salvum nunc facito | Rebelles dissipet, |
| Regem nostrum; | Et reprimat; |
| Sit læta victoria | Dolos confundito; |
| Comes et gloria, | Fraudes depellito; |
| Salvum jam facito | In te sit sita spes |
|   Tu Dominum. | O! salva nos. |

Salvation, however, was not vouchsafed the Stuart dynasty. Before the year was out, it was King James who was sent packing, and William of Orange reigned in his stead. Then, as if to keep up the irony, the song disappeared altogether until the Pretender in 1745 attempted by the aid of his faithful Scots to regain the crown his ancestor had lost. Then the self-same musical prayer, first used, all unavailing, on behalf of James II., was revived in order to serve as the Battle Hymn of the usurper who sat on his throne. Twelve days after the proclamation of the Pretender in September, 1745, at Edinburgh, "God Save the King" was sung with tumultuous enthusiasm at Drury Lane, and from that hour to this it has held the first place among the national anthems of the world.

Twenty-one years later it was adopted as a national air in Denmark. In 1793, as Heil Dir im Siegerkrantz, it became the national anthem of Prussia. About the middle of the present century the air was fitted by C. T. Brooks to the American National Anthem, "America," beginning: —

> God bless our native land!
> Firm may she ever stand,
> Through storm and might.

"God Save the Queen" is hackneyed by too much use, especially by its abuse as the signal for the close of a performance, which is almost as great a profanation as if one should use the Royal Standard as a handkerchief. But no abuse of this kind can impair its magic power when in times of national peril it bursts from the full heart. The singing of the National Anthem, and the way in which it was sung in January, 1896, when England, left in "splendid" but dangerous "isolation," was preparing for war against envious rivals in Europe and America, did more than anything else to impress the foreign observer with the intensity and depth of the national emotion. It was magnificent, almost awful, to hear the swelling notes as they rose from great congregations. It was a kind of semi-articulate expression of the deeper feelings usually unexpressed by John Bull. Only when the menace of war rouses the nation is there sufficient force to strike these sonorous chords of patriotic passion. For more than a hundred years, whenever the English people have been really stirred by imminence of national danger, or by exultation over national triumph, the most satisfying expression for their inmost aspirations has been found in the simple but vigorous verses. This is the only war-song of the modern Englishman. For him it has superseded all others, ancient or modern. "Rule Britannia" is not to be compared with it for universality of use, or for satisfying completeness of music and verse. And no part of this Battle Hymn of the British Monarchy is more genuine and hearty than the stanza which offends many pious critics on account of the fidelity with which it reproduces the spirit of the imprecatory Psalms.

It would be idle to attempt to enumerate the occasions when this anthem has been used to body forth in audible form the sentiments that throb in the heart of the nation. Whenever any number of Englishmen find themselves fronting death, or whenever they have experienced any great deliverance, whenever they thrill with exultant pride, or nerve themselves to offer an unyielding front to adverse fate, they have used "God Save the Queen" or King, as it has been and will be again, as the natural national musical vehicle for expressing what would otherwise find no utterance. It is the melody that is always heard when our island story touches the sublimer heights or sounds the profounder depths. It is one of the living links which bind into one the past, the present and future of the English race.

There is one quite recent incident that may be mentioned. When Major Wilson with his thirty-three troopers were attacked in Matabeleland in 1894 by a force of three thousand natives, who surrounded them in the forest, they fought from early morning till well on into the afternoon. All their horses were shot early in the day, and behind their dead bodies the troopers kept up a desperate fight for three hours. Not one attempted to escape. These "men of men," as the Matabele called them, fought on till their ammunition gave out, and there was not one man left to stand or fire.

When nearly all were wounded or killed, the Induna says, they (Wilson's party) left off firing, and all that could stood up, took off their hats, and sang something, the kind of song that he (the Induna) had heard missionaries sing to the natives. Knowing Wilson as we do, says a friend of his, we are sure it was "God Save the Queen." They then fired again, until only one man was left, and almost all the ammunition gone. The Matabele had such a dread of them, that even then they did not rush in and assegai them until the last man had fallen, and were so impressed with their pluck that they did not mutilate them in any way, only stripped them. The Induna estimated that the Matabele lost eight to every one of the thirty-four white men killed, and said that Lobengula's warriors lay round the dead white men like grass. After many days Mr. Dawson found thirty-three skulls lying within a circle of fifteen yards, and one skull lying thirty yards outside. He buried them under a wooden cross, inscribed, "To Brave Men." Mr. Rhodes afterwards had their remains interred in the prehistoric temple of Zimbabye, which is to be the Westminster Abbey of South Africa. It was of this incident that Mary Georges wrote—

> They sang — the white men sang —
> Sang in the face of death,
> And the forest echoes rang
> With their triumphant breath.
>
> On our spirit falleth a mighty dread;
> We feared them most when we left them dead!

## 11—GOD BLESS OUR NATIVE LAND.

For those who object on religious grounds to pray for the destruction of their enemies, also for those who prefer to pray for themselves rather than for their Sovereign, the following variant has been prepared, and is used in ordinary times. But when the shrill clarion sounds the 'larum of war, the original version holds the field:—

> GOD bless our native land!
> May heaven's protecting hand
> Still guard our shore;
> May Peace her power extend,
> Foe be transformed to friend,
> And Britain's rights depend
> On war no more.
>
> May just and righteous laws
> Uphold the public cause
> And bless our isle.
> Home of the brave and free,
> The land of liberty,
> We pray that still on thee
> Kind heaven may smile.
>
> And not this land alone,
> But be Thy mercies known
> From shore to shore.
> Lord, make the nations see
> That men should brothers be,
> And form one family,
> The wide world o'er.
>
> TUNE—"THE NATIONAL ANTHEM."

## 12—GOD SAVE THE PEOPLE.

THIS democratic anthem of the masses is much in vogue in Labour churches, Pleasant Sunday Afternoon meetings, and Congregational churches of the more advanced type. The tune to which it is set, aptly fitted to the words, has a great hold upon those who sing it. The hymn was the handiwork of Ebenezer

Elliott, the Sheffield Corn Law Rhymer, a sturdy, uncompromising Democrat, with a heart embittered against the landed classes, whose chief aim in making laws in those days seemed to him to be keeping up the price of bread, regardless of the needs of the hungry poor. But the whirligig of time brings about strange revenges, and the Sheffield which in the rough, rude rhymes of Ebenezer Elliott doomed the Protectionist to perdition now returns Col. Howard Vincent to Parliament to champion Protection masked as Fair Trade.

WHEN wilt Thou save the people?
   O God of mercy, when?
Not kings alone, but nations?
   Not thrones and crowns, but men?
Flowers of Thy heart, O God, are they:
Let them not pass, like weeds, away —
Their heritage a sunless day.
     God save the people!

Shall crime bring crime for ever,
   Strength aiding still the strong?
Is it Thy will, O Father,
   That man shall toil for wrong?
"No," say Thy mountains; "No," Thy skies;
Man's clouded sun shall brightly rise,
And songs ascend instead of sighs:
     God save the people!

When wilt Thou save the people?
   O God of mercy, when?
The people, Lord, the people,
   Not thrones and crowns, but men?
God save the people, Thine they are,
Thy children, as Thine angels fair;
From vice, oppression, and despair,
     God save the people!

      TUNE — "COMMONWEALTH."

It is the nearest approach to an English Marseillaise that a sense of social injustice has wrung from the heart of the oppressed.

The Rev. Charles Garrett, of Liverpool, writes: "This hymn rings in my mind like the cry of a nation on its knees." A Scottish journalist, writing from South Wales, says: "So far as my experience goes, this hymn can rouse great popular audiences as nothing else can. It seems to go right down to the hearts of the people, and it can be sung very effectively."

## 13—AMERICA.

IN days of peace and prosperity, through the crisis of the Civil War, and on most public occasions since the war, this hymn has gradually won recognition as a national one without the ceremonial of adoption in any historic scene. The author of the words, the Rev. Samuel Francis Smith, D.D., says of their origin: "The song was written at Andover during my student life there, I think in the winter of 1831-32. It was first used publicly at a Sunday-school celebration of July 4, in the Park Street Church, Boston." It was, indeed, an attempt to give "God Save the King" the ring of American republican patriotism. Public-school teachers throughout the United States find it most helpful in awakening a love for and a pride in the new country among the heterogeneous mass of child immigrants that must be welded into patriotic American citizens. The well-known missionary hymn, "The Morning Light is breaking," was also written at Andover at about the same date. To the author, his class-mate Oliver Wendell Holmes refers in the lines:—

"And there's a nice fellow of excellent pith,
Fate tried to conceal him by naming him Smith."

MY country! 't is of thee,
    Sweet land of Liberty,
Of thee I sing;

Land where my fathers died;
Land of the Pilgrims' pride;
From ev'ry mountain side,
  Let freedom ring.

My native country! thee,
Land of the noble free,
  Thy name I love;
I love thy rocks and rills,
Thy woods and templed hills,
My heart with rapture thrills
  Like that above.

Let music swell the breeze,
And ring among the trees
  Sweet freedom's song:
Let mortal tongues awake,
Let all that breathe partake,
Let rocks their silence break,
  The sound prolong.

Our fathers' God! to Thee,
Author of Liberty!
  To Thee we sing;
Long may our land be bright
With freedom's holy light,
Protect us by thy might,
  Great God, our King!

## 14—THE MARSEILLAISE.

ON the 5th July, 1792, when Revolutionary France was menaced with destruction by internal treason and external war,—the latter taking tangible shape in the person of the Duke of Brunswick and 80,000 Prussians, Hessians, and the royalist émigrés,—the Marseilles municipality mustered 517 men of the rank and file, with captains of fifties and of tens, 600 in all, and bade them "March, strike down the tyrant." Without an arrangement, or station, or ration, these black-browed Marseillese "who knew how to die" made their way for 600 miles across France to Paris. "The thought which works voiceless in this black-browed mass, an inspired Tyrtæan Colonel, Rouget de Lille, has translated into grim melody and rhythm, in his Hymn or March of the Marseillese, luckiest musical composition ever promulgated, the sound of which will make the blood tingle in men's veins, and whole armies and assemblages will sing it, with eyes weeping and burning, with hearts defiant of Death, Despot, and Devil." For which indeed France had not long to wait, for on Nov. 6, 1792, when Dumouriez smote the Austrians at Jemappes, it was recognised that in the Marseilles a new power had descended from above upon the French armies, and that henceforth and for many years to come they were invincible. Carlyle writes thus of that memorable day. Dumouriez, overrunning the Netherlands, came upon the Austrians at Jemappes, near Mons:—

"And fire-hail is whistling far and wide there, the great guns playing and the small; so many green heights getting fringed and maned with red fire. And Dumouriez is swept back on this wing, and swept back on that, and is like to be swept back utterly; when he rushes up in person, the prompt Polymetis, speaks a prompt word or two, and then, with clear tenor-pipe, 'uplifts the Hymn of the Marseillaise.' *entonna la Marseillaise*, ten thousand tenor or bass pipes joining; or say, some forty thousand in all, for every heart leaps at the sound; and so, with rhythmic march-melody, waxing ever quicker to double and to treble quick, they rally, they advance, they rush, death-defying, man-devouring; carry batteries, redoutes, whatsoever is to be carried; and like the fire-whirlwind, sweep all manner of Austrians from the scene of action. Thus, through the hands of Dumouriez, may Rouget de Lille, in figurative speech, be said to have gained miraculously, like another Orpheus, by his Marseillese fiddle-strings (*fidi-*

*ous canoris*), a victory of Jemappes, and conquered the Low Countries."

From that moment the Marseillaise became the National Anthem of France. All through the Napoleonic wars her armies marched to the music of Rouget de Lille, which made the tour of Europe with the eagles of France. Afterwards it became a proscribed hymn, and was, in consequence, all the more cherished. Whenever revolution burst out, her first note was ever sounded by the Marseillaise. During the Second Empire it was proscribed until the march on Berlin, which was to end at Sedan, when the Emperor permitted the nation he had betrayed once again to hear the stirring strains in which, for nearly a hundred years, its patriotic passion had vibrated through Europe. Not even the Marseillaise could avert Sedan, but it was to the music of the Marseillaise that the Empire was overthrown, and it remains to this day — Russian alliance notwithstanding — the National Hymn of the French Republic.

ALLONS, enfants de la Patrie,
Le jour de gloire est arrivé!
Contre nous de la tyrannie
L'Étendard sanglant est levé. (*bis*)
Entendez-vous dans les campagnes
Mugir ces féroces soldats?
Ils viennent jusque dans vos bras
Égorger vos fils, vos compagnes.
    Aux armes, citoyens, formez vos bataillons!
    Marchons, marchons!
    Qu'un sang impur abreuve nos sillons.

Que veut cette horde d'esclaves,
De traîtres, de rois conjurés?
Pour qui ces ignobles entraves,
Ces fers dès longtemps préparés? (*bis*)
Français, pour nous, ah! quel outrage!

Quel transport il doit exciter !
C'est nous qu'on ose menacer
De rendre à l'antique esclavage !
    Aux armes, citoyens (etc.).

Quoi, ces cohortes étrangères
Feraient la loi dans nos foyers !
Quoi, des phalanges mercenaires
Terrasseraient nos fiers guerriers ! (*bis*)
Grand Dieu ! par des mains enchaînées
Nos fronts sous le joug se ploîraient ?
De vils despotes deviendraient
Les maîtres de nos destinées ?
    Aux armes, citoyens (etc.).

Tremblez, tyrans ! et vous, perfides,
L'opprobre de tous les partis,
Tremblez ! vos projets parricides
Vont enfin recevoir leur prix. (*bis*)
Tout est soldat pour vous combattre
S'ils tombent, nos jeunes héros,
La terre en produit de nouveaux
Contre vous tout prêts à se battre.
    Aux armes, citoyens (etc.).

Français, en guerriers magnanimes,
Portez ou retenez vos coups !
Épargnez ces tristes victimes
A regret s'armant contre nous. (*bis*)
Mais les despotes sanguinaires,
Mais les complices de Bouillé,
Tous ces tigres qui, sans pitié,
Déchirent le sein de leur mère !
    Aux armes, citoyens (etc.).

Nous entrerons dans la carrière,
Quand nos aînés n'y seront plus ;

Nous y trouverons leur poussière
Et la trace de leurs vertus. (*bis*)
Bien moins jaloux de leur survivre
Que de partager leur cercueil,
Nous aurons le sublime orgueil
De les venger ou de les suivre.
    Aux armes, citoyens (etc.).

Amour sacré de la patrie,
Conduis, soutiens nos bras vengeurs.
Liberté, liberté chérie,
Combats avec tes défenseurs. (*bis*)
Sous nos drapeaux que la victoire
Accoure à tes mâles accents !
Que tes ennemis expirants
Voient ton triomphe et notre gloire !
    Aux armes, citoyens (etc.).

The Marseillaise is often sung in England, but seldom beyond the first verse, excepting in French. The English free — very free — rendering, that is sometimes used, begins thus: —

Ye sons of France, awake to glory!
  Hark! hark! what myriads bid you rise!
Your children, wives, and grandsires hoary, —
  Behold their tears and hear their cries!
Shall hateful tyrants, mischief breeding,
  With hireling hosts, a ruffian band,
  Affright and desolate the land,
While liberty and peace lie bleeding?
  To arms! to arms! ye brave!
    The avenging sword unsheathe!
  March on! march on! all hearts resolved
    On victory or death!

Outside France the Marseillaise is, however, almost exclusively monopolised by Socialist or other exponents of popular discontent. In France, of course, it is the official anthem, which is played even in the presence of Tsars. But if ever there was a hymn that helped men, the Marseillaise is that hymn. It helped millions to conquer and to die; and so, although it can hardly be regarded as an ordinary hymn, it is such an extraordinary one as to well deserve a place in this collection.

## 15 — LUTHER'S HYMN.

A BATTLE hymn, indeed, is this famous hymn which Heinrich Heine rightly describes as "the Marseillaise Hymn of the Reformation." Luther composed it for the Diet of Spires, when, on April 20, 1529, the German princes made their formal protest against the revocation of their liberties, and so became known as Protestants. In the life-and-death struggle that followed, it was as a clarion summoning all faithful souls to do battle, without fear, against the insulting foe. Luther sang it to the lute every day. It was the spiritual and national tonic of Germany, administered in those dolorous times as doctors administer quinine to sojourners in fever-haunted marshes. Every one sang it, old and young, children in the street, soldiers on the battlefield. The more heavily hit they were, the more tenaciously did they cherish the song that assured them of ultimate victory. When Melancthon and his friends, after Luther's death, were sent into banishment, they were marvellously cheered as they entered Weimar on hearing a girl sing Luther's hymn in the street. "Sing on, dear daughter mine," said Melancthon; "thou knowest not what comfort thou bringest to our heart." Nearly a hundred years later, before the great victory which he gained over the Catholic forces at Leipsic, Gustavus Adolphus asked his warriors to sing Luther's hymn, and after the victory he thanked God that He had made good the promise, "The field He will maintain it." It was sung at the Battle of Lützen. It was sung also many a time and oft during the Franco-German war. In fact, whenever the depths of the German heart are really stirred, the sonorous strains of Luther's hymn instinctively burst forth. M. Vicomte de Voguë, one of the most brilliant of contemporary writers, in his criticism of M. Zola's "Débâcle," pays a splendid tribute to the element in the German character which finds its most articulate expression in Luther's noble psalm. M. de Voguë says that M. Zola, in his work, entirely fails to explain in what the superiority of the German army consisted. What was there in these men? Why did they conquer France? Only he who knows the answer, and dares to give it, will be able to write *the* book about the war.

"He who is so well up in all the points of the battlefield of Sedan must surely know what was to be seen and heard there on the evening of Sept. 1, 1870. It was a picture to tempt his pen, — those innumerable lines of fires starring all the valley of the Meuse, those grave and solemn chants sent out into the night by hundreds of thousands of voices. No orgy, no disorder, no relaxation of discipline; the men mounting guard under arms till the inexorable task was done; the hymns to the God of victory and the distant home, — they seemed like an army of priests coming from the sacrifice. This one picture, painted as the novelist knows how to paint in his best days, would have shown us what virtues, wanting in our own camp, had kept fortune in the service of the other."

Of English versions there have been many. That of Thomas Carlyle is generally regarded as the best.

A SURE stronghold our God is He.
   A trusty shield and weapon;
Our help He'll be, and set us free
   From every ill can happen.
      That old malicious foe
      Intends us deadly woe;
      Armed with might from Hell,
      And deepest craft as well,
On earth is not his fellow.

Through our own force we nothing can,
    Straight were we lost for ever;
But for us fights the proper Man,
    By God sent to deliver.
        Ask ye who this may be?
        Christ Jesus named is He.
        Of Sabaoth the Lord;
        Sole God to be adored;
'Tis He must win the battle.

And were the world with devils filled,
    All eager to devour us,
Our souls to fear should little yield,
    They cannot overpower us.
        Their dreaded Prince no more
        Can harm us as of yore;
        Look grim as e'er he may,
        Doomed is his ancient sway;
A word can overthrow him.

God's word for all their craft and force
    One moment will not linger:
But spite of Hell shall have its course
    'Tis written by His finger.
        And though they take our life,
        Goods, honour, children, wife;
        Yet is there profit small:
        These things shall vanish all;
The city of God remaineth.

The following is given in Julian's Dictionary of Hymnology as the earliest High German Text now accessible to us. It is that of 1531:—

    EIN' feste burg ist unser Gott,
        ein gute wehr und waffen.
    Er hilfft unns frey aus aller not

die uns ytzt hat betroffen,
  Der alt böse feind
  mit ernst ers ytzt meint,
  gros macht und viel list
  sein grausam rüstung ist,
auf erd ist nicht seins gleichen.

Mit unser macht ist nichts gethan,
  wir sind gar bald verloren;
Es streit fur uns der rechte man,
  den Gott hat selbs erkoren.
    Fragstu, wer der ist?
    er heist Jhesu Christ
    der Herr Zebaoth,
    und ist kein ander Gott,
das felt mus er behalten.

Und wenn die welt vol Teuffell wehr
  und wolt uns gar vorschlingen
So fürchten wir uns nicht zu sehr
  es sol uns doch gelingen.
    Der Fürst dieser welt,
    wie sawr er sich stellt.
    thut er unns doch nicht,
    das macht, er ist gericht,
ein wörtlin kan yhn fellen.

Das wort sie sollen lassen stahn
  und kein danck dazu haben,
Er ist bey unns wol auff dem plan
  mit seinem geist und gaben.
    Nemen sie den leib,
    gut, eher, kindt unnd weib
    las faren dahin,
    sie habens kein gewin,
das reich mus uns doch bleiben.

TUNE — "WORMS," ALSO CALLED "EIN' FESTE BURG."

The Forty-sixth Psalm was always a great stand-by for fighting men. The Huguenots and Covenanters used to cheer their hearts in the extremity of adverse fortunes by the solemn chant

> God is our refuge and our strength,
>   In straits a present aid;
> Therefore, although the earth remove,
>   We will not be afraid.

It will be noted that although Luther's Hymn is suggested by the Forty-sixth Psalm, it is really Luther's Psalm, not David's. Only the idea of the stronghold is taken from the Scripture, the rest is Luther's own, "made in Germany," indeed, and not only so, but one of the most potent influences that have contributed to the making of Germany. And who knows how soon again we may see the fulfilment of Heine's speculation, when Germans "may soon have to raise again these old words, flashing and pointed with iron"? That M. de Vogüé does not stray beyond his book there is ample evidence to prove. For instance, Cassell's History of the Franco-German war describes how, the day after the battle of Sedan, a multitude of German troops, who were on the march for Paris, found it impossible to sleep, wearied though they were. They were billeted in the Parish Church of Augecourt. The excitement of the day had been too great; the memory of the bloody fight and their fallen comrades mingled strangely with pride of victory and the knowledge that they had rescued their country from the foe. Suddenly in the twilight and the stillness a strain of melody proceeded from the organ, — at first softly, very softly, and then with ever-increasing force, — the grand old hymn-tune, familiar as "household words" to every German ear, "Nun danket alle Gott," swelled along the vaulted aisles. With one voice officers and men joined in the holy strains; and when the hymn was ended, the performer, a simple villager, came forward and delivered a short, simple, heartfelt speech. Then, turning again to the organ, he struck up Luther's old hymn, "Ein' feste Burg ist unser Gott," and again all joined with heart and voice. The terrible strain on their system, which had tried their weary souls and had banished slumber from their eyes, was now removed, and they laid themselves down with thankful hearts and sought and found the rest they so much needed.

Frederick the Great on one occasion called Luther's Hymn "God Almighty's Grenadier March."

## 16—GUSTAVUS ADOLPHUS'S BATTLE HYMN.

FEW figures stand out so visibly against the bloody mist of the religious wars of the seventeenth century as that of Gustavus Adolphus, the hero-king of Sweden, who triumphed at Leipsic and who fell dead on the morning of victory at Lützen. The well-known hymn beginning "Verzage nicht, du Häuflein," which is known as Gustavus Adolphus's Battle Hymn, was composed by Pastor Altenburg, at Erfurt, on receiving the news of the great victory of Leipsic, which gave fresh heart and hope to the Protestants of Germany. It was sung on the morning of the Battle of Lützen, under the following circumstances: When the morning of Nov. 16, 1632, dawned, the Catholic and Protestant armies under Wallenstein and Gustavus Adolphus stood facing each other. Gustavus ordered all his chaplains to hold a service of prayer. He threw himself upon his knees and prayed fervently while the whole army burst out into a lofty song of praise and prayer,

"Verzage nicht, du Häuflein klein."

As they prayed and sang a mist descended, through which neither army could discern the foe. The King set his troops in battle-array, giving them as their watchword, "God with us." As he rode along the lines, he ordered the kettle-drums and trumpets to strike up Luther's hymns, "Ein' feste Burg" and "Es wollt uns Gott genädig sein." As they played, the soldiers joined in as with one voice. The mist began to lift, the sun shone bright, and Gustavus knelt again in prayer. Then rising, he cried: "Now we will set to, please God," and then louder he said, "Jesu, Jesu, Jesu, help me this day to fight for the honour of Thy name!" Then he charged the enemy at full speed, defended only by a leathern gorget. "God is my harness," he replied to his servant, who rushed to put on his armour. The battle was hot and bloody. At eleven in the forenoon the fatal bullet struck Gustavus, and he sank dying from his horse, crying, "My God, my God!" The combat went on for hours afterwards, but when twilight fell Wallenstein's army broke and fled, and the dead king remained victor of the field on which with his life he had purchased the religious liberties of Northern Europe.

FEAR not, O little flock, the foe,
   Who madly seeks your overthrow,
  Dread not his rage and power;
What, tho' your courage sometimes faints,
His seeming triumph o'er God's saints
  Lasts but a little hour.

Be of good cheer, — your cause belongs
To Him who can avenge your wrongs,
  Leave it to Him, our Lord.
Tho' hidden yet from all our eyes,
He sees the Gideon who shall rise
  To save us, and his word.

As true as God's own word is true,
Nor earth, nor hell, with all their crew,
  Against us shall prevail, —
A jest and byword are they grown;
"*God is with us,*" we are His own,
  Our victory cannot fail.

Amen, Lord Jesus, grant our prayer!
Great Captain, now Thine arm make bare;
  Fight for us once again!
So shall Thy saints and martyrs raise
A mighty chorus to Thy praise,
  World without end. Amen.

## 17 — THE BATTLE HYMN OF THE REPUBLIC.

MINE eyes have seen the glory of the coming of the Lord;
He is trampling out the vintage where the grapes of wrath are stored;
He hath loosed the fateful lightning of his terrible swift sword;
  His truth is marching on.

I have seen Him in the watch-fires of a hundred circling camps;
They have builded Him an altar in the evening dews and damps;
I have read His righteous sentence by the dim and flaring lamps;
  His Day is marching on.

I have read a fiery gospel writ in burnished rows of steel —
"As ye deal with My contemners, so with you My grace shall deal;"
Let the Hero born of woman crush the serpent with His heel,
  Since God is marching on.

He has sounded forth the trumpet that shall never call retreat;
He is sifting out the hearts of men before His judgment-seat;

Oh! be swift, my soul, to answer Him; be jubilant, my feet,—
> Our God is marching on.

In the beauty of the lilies Christ was born across the sea,
With a glory in His bosom that transfigures you and me;
As He died to make men holy, let us die to make men free,
> While God is marching on,
>> TUNE — "JOHN BROWN'S BODY."

This splendid Battle Hymn of the Republic was written by Julia Ward Howe on the outbreak of the American war, 1860.

John Habberton, writing long after it was all over, says:—

"The old air has a wonderful influence over me. I heard it in Western camp meetings and negro cabins when I was a boy. I saw the 22nd Massachusetts march down Broadway singing the same air during a rush to the front during the early days of the war; I have heard it sung by warrior tongues in nearly every Southern State; my old brigade sang it softly, but with a swing that was terrible in its earnestness, as they lay behind their stacks of arms just before going into action; I have heard it played over the grave of many a dead comrade; the semi-mutinous —th cavalry became peaceful and patriotic again as their bandmaster played the old air, after having asked permission to try his hand on them; it is the tune that burst forth spontaneously in our barracks on that glorious morning when we learned that the war was over, and it was sung with words adapted to the occasion by some good rebel friends of mine on our first social meeting after the war."

## 18 — CROMWELL'S BATTLE PSALMS.

THE most famous of the Battle Songs of the Ironsides was the Sixty-eighth Psalm, which was sung before fighting, and the One Hundred and Seventeenth, which they sang after victory. They had no need for anything to sing after defeat, for they never were defeated.

The Sixty-eighth was a famous warrior-psalm long before Cromwell's time. It was the favourite of Charlemagne. Savonarola chanted it as he trod the dolorous way to the stake. It was called by the Huguenots the Song of Battles, and was raised by them in many a desperate fight. The most notable occasion on which it was sung by the Army of the Commonwealth was on the morning of the Battle of Dunbar. Terrible indeed, in the dim and misty morning, must have sounded the voices of the Ironsides singing as they stood ready waiting for the word to charge. This was probably the version that they used:—

LET God arise, and scattered
   let all his en'mies be;
And let all those that do him hate
   before his presence flee.

As smoke is driv'n, so drive thou them;
   as fire melts wax away,
Before God's face let wicked men
   so perish and decay.

But let the righteous be glad:
   let them before God's sight
Be very joyful: yea, let them
   rejoice with all their might.

To God sing, to his name sing praise;
   extol him with your voice,
That rides on heav'n, by his name
   before his face rejoice.

The One Hundred and Seventeenth Psalm was sung after the victory was won, and became known thereafter as the Dunbar Psalm.

When "the Scotch army, shivered to utter ruin, rushes in tumultuous wreck," "the Lord General made a halt, and sung the one hundred and seventeenth psalm, till our horse could gather for the chase." "Hundred and seventeenth psalm," says Mr. Carlyle, "at the foot of the Doon Hill; there we uplift it, to the tune of Bangor, or some still higher score, and roll it strong and great against the sky":—

O GIVE ye praise unto the Lord,
    all nations that be;
Likewise, ye people all, accord
    his name to magnify.

For great to us-ward ever are
    his loving-kindnesses:
His truth endures for evermore.
    The Lord O do ye bless.

Doggerel, no doubt; but who would exchange that rugged verse, sung from the hearts of the victors of Dunbar, while the smoke of their powder was still lying low over the dead, for the most mellifluous verse whose melody charmed the ear of the critic, but never stirred the mighty hearts of heroes?

## 19—GARIBALDI'S HYMN.

The Rev. H. R. Haweis, who probably is the best repository of Garibaldian reminiscences among English-speaking men, has been good enough to send me the following notes on the way in which this famous hymn helped the Italian struggle for national unity and independence. Mr. Haweis writes:—

"Garibaldi's hymn, like so many other tunes and stanzas, was composed by a comparatively obscure person named Luigi Mercantini, and the music was composed by Alessio Olivieri, of Genoa. I well remember in 1860 being told by an Italian how a friend of his had taken him into a back shop in Venice for fear of the Austrians, and played over to him the then unknown tune, showing him the words to which it was to be sung, and declaring that it would be likely to seize upon the popular heart and ear and become the clarion of patriotic advance and victory. This turned out to be the case. Throughout the length and breadth of Italy — from '59 to '69, at all events — Garibaldi's hymn rang out in every café, on every organ, at every social or political gathering, and in every street throughout Italy. It is lively and buoyant. Why it is called a hymn it is difficult to say — it has a bounce and go about it which suggests the irrepressible recklessness, fearlessness, and audacious jollity of youth. It voiced young Italy's aspirations. The revolution was indeed the work chiefly of boys with a few veterans at their backs. The 1000 of Marsala, the remnants of the Italian legion, formed in South America and the defenders of Rome in 1848 — these were the iron-handed, golden-souled veterans — and the Garibaldian armies were recruited from the boys of Italy. Garibaldi's hymn suited them down to the ground. It ranks with the Marseillaise as a revolutionary inspirer, but it has a light-hearted joyousness and a rollicking rush and devil-may-care slapdash about it that the gloomier Marseillaise cannot lay claim to. I shall never forget coming down one fresh autumn morning from the Camaldoli hills above Naples and meeting about one hundred Garibaldians in their red shirts and muskets shouldered marching joyously up hill — it was a few days after the battle of Volturno — four trumpeters walked in front, blowing Garibaldi's hymn to their hearts' content, whilst the young lithe guerilleros (I don't think there could have been one over twenty) seemed to step on air. I can recollect their bright sunny faces and eyes glowing with happy enthusiasm even now — lack-a-day, 't is thirty-six years ago!"

SI scopron le tombe, si levano i morti,
   I martiri nostri son tutti risorti!
   Le spade nel pugno, gli allori alle chiome,
   La fiamma ed il nome d'Italia sul cor!
Veniamo! Veniamo! su, o giovani schiere!
   Su al vento per tutto le nostre bandiere!
   Su tutti col ferro, su tutti col foco,
   Su tutti col foco d'Italia nei cor.
            Va fuora d'Italia, va fuora ch'è l'ora,
            Va fuora d'Italia, va fuora, o stranier.

La terra dei fiori, dei suoni e dei carmi
   Ritorni quai era la terra dell'armi!
   Di cento catene ci avvinser la mano,
   Ma ancor di Legnano sa i ferri brandir.
Bastone tedesco l'Italia non doma,
   Non crescon al giogo le stirpi di Roma;
   Più Italia non vuole stranieri e tiranni,
   Già troppi son gli anni che dura il servir.
            Va fuora d'Italia, va fuora ch'è l'ora,
            Va fuora d'Italia, va fuora, o stranier.

Le case d'Italia son fatte per noi,
   È là sul Danubio la casa de' tuoi;
   Tu i camoi ci guasti, tu il pane c'involi,
   I nostri figliuoli per noi li vogliam.
Son l'Alpi e i due mari d'Italia i confini,
   Col carro di foco rompiam gli Apennini;
   Distrutto ogni segno di vecchia frontiera,
   La nostra bandiera per tutto innalziam.
            Va fuora d'Italia, va fuora ch'è l'ora,
            Va fuora d'Italia, va fuora, o stranier.

Sien mute le lingue, sien pronte le braccia;
   Soltanto al nimico volgiamo la faccia,
   E tosto oltre i monti n'andrà lo straniero,
   Se tutta un pensiero l'Italia sarà.

Non basta il trionfo di barbare spoglie,
　Si chiudan ai ladri d'Italia le soglie;
　Le genti d'Italia son tutte una sola,
　Son tutte una sola le cento città.
　　　Va fuora d'Italia, va fuora ch'è l'ora,
　　　Va fuora d'Italia, va fuora, o stranier.

Se ancora dell'Alpi tentasser gli spaldi,
　Il grido *d'all'armi* darà Garibaldi;
　E s'arma allo squillo, che vien da Caprera,
　Dei mille la schiera che l'Etna assaltò.
E dietro alla rossa vanguardia dei bravi
　Si muovon d'Italia le tende e le navi;
　Già ratto sull'orma del fido guerriero
　L'ardente destriero Vittorio spronò.
　　　Va fuora d'Italia, va fuora ch'è l'ora,
　　　Va fuora d'Italia, va fuora, o stranier.

Per sempre è caduto degli empi l'orgoglio,
　A dir-viva Italia-va il Re in Campidoglio,
　La Senna e il Tamigi saluta ed onora
　L'antica signora che torna a regnar.
Contenta del regno fra l'isole e i monti
　Soltanto ai tiranni minaccia le fronti;
　Dovunque le genti percuota un tiranno
　Suoi figli usciranno per terra e per mar.
　　　Va fuora d'Italia, va fuora ch'è l'ora,
　　　Va fuora d'Italia, va fuora, o stranier.

A friend has kindly sent me the following free translation of the first stanza:—

> Uplifted the tombstones!
> Our martyrs arisen!
> Brave Italy's bravest
> Have leapt from Death's prison!

Fair bays on each forehead,
Each hand with its steel,
Hearts beating and burning
    For Italy's weal.

Up! up! oh my brothers,
And chase from our land
The foeman, the alien,
With sword and with brand!
Wave, wave your bright banners
The while glad and high
Throb hearts that so proudly
    For Italy die!

## III. — Ancient Hymns.

### 20 — THE MAGNIFICAT.

THE song of the Virgin Mary on learning that she was to be the mother of the Messiah takes precedence of all other hymns of the Church. There is a curiously persistent note in it, of the exaltation of the humble, and the humiliation of the powerful, that must have sounded ill in the ears of the monarchs and nobles and champions of the constituted order. It is peculiarly fitting that this revolutionary pæan of gratitude should be adopted by the Church from the lips of a woman, for, as any one may discover who cares to look facts in the face, or even to read such a text-book as Mill's "Subjection of Women," woman, after all these centuries, is still everywhere awaiting the fulfilment of the promise — "deposuit potentes de sede, et exaltavit humiles."

MY soul doth magnify the Lord,
    And my spirit hath rejoiced in God my Saviour.

For he hath regarded the low estate of his handmaiden: for, behold, from henceforth all generations shall call me blessed.

For he that is mighty hath done to me great things; and holy *is* his name.

And his mercy *is* on them that fear him from generation to generation.

He hath showed strength with his arm; he hath scattered the proud in the imagination of their hearts.

He hath put down the mighty from *their* seats, and exalted them of low degree.

He hath filled the hungry with good things; and the rich he hath sent empty away.

He hath holpen his servant Israel, in remembrance of *his* mercy;

As he spake to our fathers, to Abraham, and to his seed for ever.

MAGNIFICAT: anima mea Dominum.
Et exultavit spiritus meus: in Deo salutari meo.

Quia respexit humilitatem ancillæ suæ: ecce enim ex hoc beatam me dicent omnes generationes.

Quia fecit mihi magna qui potens est: et sanctum nomen ejus.

Et misericordia ejus a progenie in progenies: timentibus eum.

Fecit potentiam in brachio suo: dispersit superbos mente cordis sui.

Deposuit potentes de sede: et exaltavit humiles.

Esurientes implevit bonis: et divites dimisit inanes.

Suscepit Israel puerum suum: recordatus misericordiæ suæ.

Sicut locutus est ad patres nostros: Abraham, et semini ejus in sæcula.

Gloria Patri, etc.

## 21 — GLORIA IN EXCELSIS.

After the Magnificat, this may properly be regarded as the earliest Christian hymn. It is built up as from a foundation upon the angels' song which the shepherds heard who were keeping their flocks by night when Jesus was born in Bethlehem of Judæa. But the anthem that sufficed for the angels at the Nativity was soon found inadequate for the Church that worshipped the Crucified. Hence the evolution of the Gloria, which by the end of the fifth century had been developed into the hymn which, with variations in one clause, is used alike by Greek, Latin, and Protestant believers all over the world. The text is here given in Latin and English. The Greeks say instead of "O Lord, the only begotten Son, Jesus Christ," "Lord, the only begotten Son, Jesus Christ and Holy Spirit."

GLORY be to God on high, and in earth peace, good-will towards men.

We praise Thee, we bless Thee, we worship Thee, we glorify Thee.

We give thanks to Thee, for Thy great glory.

O Lord God, heavenly King, God the Father Almighty,

O Lord, the only begotten Son, Jesus Christ,

O Lord God, Lamb of God, Son of the Father,

That takest away the sins of the world, have mercy upon us.

Thou that takest away the sins of the world, have mercy upon us.

Thou that takest away the sins of the world, receive our prayer.

Thou that sittest at the right hand of God the Father, have mercy upon us.

For Thou only art holy, Thou only art the Lord.

Thou only, O Christ, with the Holy Ghost, art most high in the glory of God the Father. Amen.

GLORIA in excelsis Deo. Et in terra pax hominibus bonæ voluntatis.
Laudamus te. Benedicimus te. Adoramus te. Glorificamus te.
Gratias agimus tibi propter magnam gloriam tuam. [potens.
Domine Deus, Rex cælestis, Deus Pater omni-
Domine Fili unigenite Jesu Christe.
Domine Deus. Agnus Dei, Filius Patris.
Qui tollis peccata mundi, miserere nobis.
Qui tollis peccata mundi, suscipe deprecationem nostram.
Qui sedes ad dexteram Patris, miserere nobis.
Quoniam tu solus sanctus. Tu solus Dominus.
Tu solus altissimus Jesu Christe. Cum sancto Spiritu, in gloria Dei Patris. Amen.

This hymn is believed to have been the morning song of the Christians in primitive days, — the hymn sung by the martyrs as the day dawned on which they were to be butchered, to make a Roman holiday. For nearly nineteen centuries it spans the history of our race with a ray of melody and light. This hymn has helped indeed.

## 22 — NUNC DIMITTIS.

Simeon's song of thankfulness on seeing the infant Christ has been frequently paraphrased, but the non-metrical version is most used and best known.

LORD, now lettest Thou Thy servant depart in peace: according to Thy word.
For mine eyes have seen Thy salvation.
Which Thou hast prepared before the face of all people.
A light to lighten the Gentiles: and the glory of Thy people Israel.
Glory be to the Father, etc.

*Ant.* Salva nos.

NUNC dimittis servum tuum, Domine : * secundum verbum tuum in pace.

Quia viderunt oculi mei * salutare tuum.

Quod parasti * ante faciem omnium populorum.

Lumen ad revelationem gentium,* et gloriam plebis tuæ Israel.

Gloria Patri.

*Ant.* Salva nos, Domine, vigilantes, custodi nos dormientes: ut vigilemus cum Christo, et requiescamus in pace.

## 23 — THE CANDLE-LIGHT HYMN.

THE Evening Hymn, the Phos Hilaron, quoted by St. Basil in the fourth century, dates from the first or second century. As the Gloria was the Christian's salute to the rising sun, so the Phos Hilaron was sung at eventide when the time of the lighting of lamps had come. It is still used as the Vesper Hymn in the Greek churches. The following is Keble's translation : —

HAIL, gladdening Light, of His pure glory pour'd
Who is the Immortal Father, Heavenly, Blest,
Holiest of Holies, Jesus Christ, our Lord.
   Now we are come to the sun's hour of rest,
     The lights of evening round us shine,
We hymn the Father, Son, and Holy Spirit Divine.

   Worthiest art Thou at all times to be sung
     With undefilèd tongue,
Son of our God, Giver of life, Alone !
Therefore in all the world Thy glories, Lord, they own. Amen.

## 24—THE HYMN OF THE CATACOMBS.

Those who have wandered through any part of the ten miles of the labyrinth known as the Catacombs of Calixtus, which are said to contain the remains of a million Christian dead, will be familiar with the constant, almost infantile, persistence of the reference to Christ in inscriptions. Whether it is the dove, or the palm, or the fish, or the sacred monogram, it is always Jesus Christ, Son of God, Saviour. They had fallen in love with Jesus of Nazareth, had these hunted Christians, and they carved his name everywhere, or his symbol, as the lovelorn Orlando chiselled Rosalind's name on the bark of the trees in the forest of Ardennes. From these early days, when for the first time the human heart felt the fresh gush of passionate love for the Divine, made Man in order to become the Heavenly Bridegroom of his Spouse of the Church, there has come down to us little in the shape of authentic song save that hymn which, versified as the hymn "Shepherd of Tender Youth," is still to be heard in our churches to-day. But how different the circumstances of the modern congregation and those under which the little flock of the persecuted mustered in the black subterranean City of the Dead to enjoy the ecstasy of singing to Him whose love made the horrors of the torture-chamber and the shame of the Colosseum sweeter than all the honours and glories of the world. "Nowhere," says Zola, in his masterly picture of Rome, "had there been more intimate and touching life than in these buried cities of the unknown lowly dead, so gentle, so beautiful, and so chaste. And a mighty breath had formerly come from them, the breath of a new humanity destined to renew the world. With the advent of meekness, contempt of the flesh, relinquishment of terrestrial joys, and a passion for death, which delivers and opens the portals of Paradise, a new world had begun." And this ancient hymn, sole survivor of many such which helped them to the hidden source of their strength, still, after all these centuries, exhales somewhat of the mystic fragrance which lingered around that mighty love by which they overcame the world. The following is the translation of Dean Plumptre:—

CURB for the stubborn steed,
   Making its will give heed;
Wing that directest right
The wild bird's wandering flight;
Helm for the ships that keep
Their pathway o'er the deep;
Shepherd of sheep that own
Their Master on the Throne,
Stir up Thy children meek
With guileless lips to speak,
In hymn and song Thy praise,
Guide of their infant ways.
O King of saints, O Lord,
Mighty, all-conquering Word;
Son of the highest God
Wielding His wisdom's rod;
Our stay when cares annoy,
Giver of endless joy;
Of all our mortal race
Saviour of boundless grace,
          O Jesus, hear!
Shepherd and Sower Thou,
Now helm, and bridle now,
Wing for the heavenward flight
Of flock all pure and bright,
Fisher of men, the blest,
Out of the world's unrest,
Out of Sin's troubled sea
Taking us, Lord, to Thee;
Out of the waves of strife,

With bait of blissful life,
With choicest fish, good store,
Drawing Thy nets to shore.
Lead us, O Shepherd true,
Thy mystic sheep, we sue,
Lead us, O holy Lord,
Who from Thy sons dost ward,
With all-prevailing charm,
Peril, and curse, and harm :
O path where Christ has trod,
O Way that leads to God,
O Word, abiding aye,
O endless light on high,
Mercy's fresh-springing flood.
Worker of all things good,
O glorious life of all
That on their Maker call,
         Christ Jesus, hear ;
O milk of Heaven, that prest
From full o'erflowing breast
Of her, the mystic Bride,
Thy wisdom hath supplied;
Thine infant children seek,
With baby lips, all weak,
Filled with the Spirit's dew
From that dear bosom true,
Thy praises pure to sing,
Hymns meet for Thee, our King,
         For Thee, the Christ;
Our holy tribute this,
For wisdom, life and bliss,
Singing in chorus meet,
Singing in concert sweet,
The Almighty Son.
We, heirs of peace unpriced,

We, who are born in Christ,
A people pure from stain,
Praise we our God again,
    Lord of our Peace!

## 25—"ART THOU WEARY, ART THOU LANGUID?"

THE Monastery of Mar Saba, founded before the Hegira of Mohammed, still stands on its ancient rock looking down upon the valley of the Kedron. Forty monks still inhabit the cells which cluster round the grave of St. Sabas, the founder, who died in 532, and still far below in the depths of the gorge the wolves and the jackals muster at morning light to eat the offal and refuse which the monks fling down below. In this monastic fortress lived in the eighth century a monk named Stephen, who, before he died, was gifted from on high with the supreme talent of embodying in a simple hymn so much of the essence of the Divine life that came to the world through Christ Jesus that in this last decade of the nineteenth century no hymn more profoundly touches the heart and raises the spirits of Christian worshippers. Dr. Neale paraphrased this song of Stephen the Sabaite, so that this strain, originally raised on the stern ramparts of an outpost of Eastern Christendom already threatened with submersion beneath the flood of Moslem conquest, rings with ever increasing volume of melodious sound through the whole wide world to-day.

ART thou weary, art thou languid,
  Art thou sore distrest?
"Come to Me," saith One, "and coming,
  Be at rest."

Hath He marks to lead me to Him,
  If He be my guide?
"In His feet and hands are wound-prints,
  And His side."

Is there diadem, as monarch,
  That His brow adorns?
"Yes, a crown, in very surety,
  But of thorns!"

If I find Him, if I follow,
  What His guerdon here?
"Many a sorrow, many a labour,
  Many a tear."

If I still hold closely to Him,
  What hath He at last?
"Sorrow vanquished, labour ended,
  Jordan past!"

If I ask Him to receive me,
  Will He say me nay?
"Not till earth, and not till heaven,
  Pass away!"

Finding, following, keeping, struggling,
  Is He sure to bless?
"Angels, prophets, martyrs, virgins,
  Answer, Yes!"

                TUNE — "STEPHANOS."

Mr. Duffield reminds us of a reference to a verse of this hymn which affords a bizarre but suggestive contrast to the life in the austere and secluded monastery where it first was given to the world. Mr. Duffield says:—

"Miss Sally Pratt McLean has used this hymn in her story of 'Cape Cod Folks' (p. 300). It is the duet which George Oliver and Benny Cradlebow sing together as they are mending the boat just before Cradlebow's heroic death. Captain Arkell tells of it thus:

"'By and by, him and George Oliver struck up a song. I've heern 'em sing it before, them two. As nigh as I calc'late, it's about finding rest in Jesus, and one a askin' questions, all fa'r and squar', to know the way and whether it's goin' to lead thar straight or not, and the other answerin'. And he was a tinkerin' 'way up on the foremast. George Oliver and the rest of us was astern, and I'll hear to my dyin' day how his voice came a floatin' down to us thar, — chantin' like it was, — cl'ar and fearless and slow. So he asks, for findin' Jesus, ef thar's any marks to foller by; and George, he answers about them bleedin' nail-prints, and the great one in his side. So then that voice comes down agin, askin' if thar's any crown, like other kings, to tell him by; and George, he answers straight about that crown o' thorns. Then says that other voice, floatin' so strong and cl'ar, and if he gin up all and follered, what should he have? What how? So George, he sings deep o' the trial and the sorrowin'. But that other voice never shook 'a askin', and what if he helt to him to the end, what then should it be — what then? George Oliver answers: "Forevermore, the sorrowin' ended — Death gone over." Then he sings out, like his mind was all made up, "And if he undertook it, would he likely be turned away?" "And it's likelier," George answers him, "that heaven and earth shall pass." So I'll hear it to my dyin' day, his voice a floatin' down to me from up above thar, askin' them questions that nobody could ever answer like, so soon he answered 'em for himself.'"

## 26 — VENI CREATOR SPIRITUS.

For nine hundred years this hymn has been in constant use in the West. It has been ascribed to Charlemagne, St. Ambrose, and Gregory the Great. It has been translated by Dryden, Luther, Bishop Cosin, and innumerable other singers. Ekkehard, the Monk of St. Gall, says that the groaning of a water-wheel, whose supply of water was running short, suggested to Notker, who was lying sleepless in an adjoining dormitory, the possibility of setting its melancholy moaning to music.

He succeeded so well that he produced the Sequence on the Holy Spirit, which, being sent by him to Charles (the Fat, not Charlemagne), led the latter to compose the "Veni Creator Spiritus." A strange legend as to the origin of a hymn that, among its other achievements, has the singular good fortune of being the only hymn in the English Prayer Book. Bishop Cosin's version of the hymn has been used for over two hundred years at the Consecration of Anglican bishops and priests. In the Roman Church it was appointed for use at the Creation of a Pope, the Election of a Bishop, the Coronation of Kings, and the Elevation and Translation of Saints. The Latin version is that now in use in the Roman Church. It differs slightly — chiefly in the order of the words — from the original version.

COME, Holy Ghost, our souls inspire,
And lighten with celestial fire;
Thou the anointing Spirit art,
Who dost Thy sevenfold gifts impart:
Thy blessèd unction from above
Is comfort, life, and fire of love.

Enable with perpetual light
The dullness of our blinded sight:
Anoint and cheer our soilèd face
With the abundance of Thy grace:
Keep far our foes, give peace at home;
Where Thou art Guide no ill can come.

Teach us to know the Father, Son,
And Thee, of Both, to be but One;
That through the ages all along
This may be our endless song,
  Praise to Thy eternal merit,
  Father, Son, and Holy Spirit.
                          Amen.

VENI, Creator Spiritus,
Mentes tuorum visita,
Imple superna gratia,
Quæ tu creasti pectora.

Qui diceris Paraclitus,
Altissimi donum Dei,
Fons vivus, ignis, charitas,
Et spiritalis unctio.

Tu septiformis munere,
Digitus Paternæ dexteræ,
Tu rite promissum Patris,
Sermone ditans guttura.

Accende lumen sensibus,
Infunde amorem cordibus,
Infirma nostri corporis,
Virtute firmans perpeti.

Hostem repellas longius,
Pacemque dones protinus;
Ductore sic te prævio
Vitemus omne noxium.

Per te sciamus da Patrem,
Noscamus atque Filium,
Teque utriusque Spiritum
Credamus omni tempore.

TUNE — "VENI CREATOR, NO. 1."

The Primate of Scotland says that he uses this hymn more than daily, and loves it beyond all others. Professor Barrett, speaking of his own experience, says: "There is no hymn which dwells so vividly in my memory as this, nor do I think any has been more stirring and helpful to me."

## IV.—Times and Seasons.

### 27—CHRISTMAS. ADESTE FIDELES.

THE use of this Christmas hymn only dates from the close of the last century, although it may have been composed a century earlier.

> O COME, all ye faithful,
>   Joyful and triumphant,
> O come ye, O come ye to Bethlehem;
>   Come and behold Him
>   Born, the King of Angels;
>   O come, let us adore Him,
>   O come, let us adore Him,
> O come, let us adore Him, Christ the Lord.
>
>   God of God,
>   Light of Light,
> Lo! He abhors not the Virgin's womb;
>   Very God,
>   Begotten, not created;
>   O come, let us adore Him, etc.
>
>   Sing, choirs of Angels,
>   Sing in exultation,
> Sing, all ye citizens of Heav'n above:
>   "Glory to God
>   In the highest;"
>   O come, let us adore Him, etc.
>
>   Yea, Lord, we greet Thee,
>   Born this happy morning;
> Jesu, to Thee be glory given;
>   Word of the Father,
>   Now in flesh appearing;

O come, let us adore Him,
O come, let us adore Him,
O come, let us adore Him, Christ the Lord.
Amen.

ADESTE, fidéles,
 Læti triumphántes;
Veníte, veníte in Bethlehem;
 Nátum vidéte
 Regem angelórum;
 Veníte adorémus,
 Veníte adorémus,
Veníte adorémus Dominum.

 Deum de Deo,
 Lúmen de Lúmine,
Gestant puellæ viscera:
 Deum vérum,
 Genitum non fáctum:
 Veníte adorémus, etc.

 Cantet nunc Io
 Chorus angelórum;
Cantet nunc aula cœléstium,
 Gloria in excelsis Deo:
 Veníte adorémus, etc.

 Ergo qui nátus
 Die hodiérna,
Jesu, Tibi sit glória:
 Patris aeterni
 Verbum caro factum:
 Veníte adorémus, etc.

TUNE—"ADESTE FIDELES."

## 28 — CHRISTMAS. HARK! THE HERALD ANGELS SING.

This familiar Christmas hymn was originally written, "Hark how all the welkin rings," as is shown within brackets, and also in the second verse there is a change. It is printed at the end of the Book of Common Prayer, and is the only Wesleyan hymn thus favoured. Both the hymn and the tune are inseparably associated with the English Christmas.

HARK! the herald angels sing, —
　Glory to the new-born King;
[Hark how all the welkin rings,
"Glory to the King of kings.]
Peace on earth, and mercy mild,
God and sinners reconciled!"

Joyful, all ye nations, rise,
Join the triumph of the skies;
With the angelic host proclaim,
Christ is born in Bethlehem.
[Universal Nature, say,
"Christ the Lord is born to-day!"]

Christ, by highest heaven adored,
Christ, the everlasting Lord,
Late in time behold Him come,
Offspring of a virgin's womb.

Veiled in flesh, the Godhead see,
Hail, the Incarnate Deity!
Pleased as man with men to appear,
Jesus, our Immanuel here!

Hail, the heavenly Prince of Peace!
Hail, the Sun of Righteousness!
Light and life to all He brings,
Risen with healing in His wings.

Mild He lays His glory by,
Born, that man no more may die,
Born, to raise the sons of earth,
Born, to give them second birth.

Come, Desire of Nations, come,
Fix in us Thy humble home;
Rise, the woman's conquering Seed,
Bruise in us the Serpent's head.

Now display Thy saving power,
Ruined nature now restore;
Now in mystic union join
Thine to ours, and ours to Thine.

Adam's likeness, Lord, efface,
Stamp Thy image in its place;
Second Adam from above,
Reinstate us in Thy love.

Let us Thee, though lost, regain,
Thee, the Life, the Heavenly Man:
Oh! to all Thyself impart,
Formed in each believing heart.

## 29 — LENT. MISERERE.

THE penitential psalm (the fifty-first), attributed to David after his sin with Bathsheba, is, perhaps, of all the psalms in the Psalter, that which has helped men most. Mr. Marson says, in his "Psalms at Work": "None of the other psalms have had half the effect upon men's minds that this one has had. It has a library of its own." It was the favourite of Aldhelm in the eighth century and of Keble in the nineteenth.

HAVE mercy upon me, O God, according to thy lovingkindness; according unto the multitude of thy tender mercies blot out my transgressions.

Wash me thoroughly from mine iniquity, and cleanse me from my sin.

For I acknowledge my trangressions; and my sin is ever before me.

Against thee, thee only, have I sinned, and done this evil in thy sight; that thou mightest be justified when thou speakest, and be clear when thou judgest.

Behold I was shapen in iniquity; and in sin did my mother conceive me.

Behold, thou desirest truth in the inward parts; and in the hidden part thou shalt make me to know wisdom.

Purge me with hyssop, and I shall be clean; wash me, and I shall be whiter than snow.

Make me to hear joy and gladness; that the bones which thou hast broken may rejoice.

Hide thy face from my sins, and blot out all mine iniquities.

Create in me a clean heart, O God; and renew a right spirit within me.

Cast me not away from thy presence; and take not thy holy spirit from me.

Restore unto me the joy of my salvation; and uphold me with thy free spirit.

Then will I teach transgressors thy ways; and sinners shall be converted unto thee.

Deliver me from bloodguiltiness, O God, thou God of my salvation; and my tongue shall sing aloud of thy righteousness.

O Lord, open thou my lips; and my mouth shall show forth thy praise.

For thou desirest not sacrifice; else would I give it; thou delightest not in burnt offering.

The sacrifices of God are a broken spirit; a broken and a contrite heart, O God, thou wilt not despise.

Do good in thy good pleasure unto Zion; build thou the walls of Jerusalem.

Then shalt thou be pleased with the sacrifices of righteousness, with burnt offering and whole burnt offering; then shall they offer bullocks upon thine altar.

MISERERE mei, Deus: secúndum magnam misericórdiam tuam.

Et secúndum multitúdinem miseratiónum tuárum: dele iniquitátem meam.

Amplius lava me ab iniquitáte mea: et a peccáto meo munda me.

Quoniam iniquitátem meam ego cognósco: et peccátum meum contra me est semper.

Tibi soli peccávi, et malum coram te feci: ut justificéris in sermónibus tuis, et vincas cum judicáris.

Ecce enim in iniquitátibus concéptus sum: et in peccátis concepit me mater mea.

Ecce enim, veritátem dilexísti: in cérta et occúlta sapiéntiæ tuæ, manifestásti mihi.

Aspérges me hyssópo, et mundábor: lavábis me, et super nivem dealbábor.

Audítui meo dabis gaudium et lætítiam: et exultábunt ossa humiliáta.

Avérte fáciem tuam a peccátis meis: et omnes iniquitátes meas dele.

Cor mundum crea in me, Deus: et spíritum rectum ínnova in viscéribus meis.

Ne projicias me a fácie tua: et Spíritum sanctum tuum ne aúferas a me.

Redde mihi lætitiam salutáris tui: et spíritu principáli confirma me.

Docébo iníquos vias tuas: et impii ad te converténtur.

Libera me de sanguínibus, Deus, Deus salútis meæ: et exultábit lingua mea justitiam tuam.
Domine, lábia mea apéries: et os meum annuntiábit laudem tuam.
Quoniam si voluísses sacrifícium, dedissem, utique: holocaústis non delectáberis.
Sacrifícium Deo spíritus contribulátus: cor contrítum et humiliátum, Deus, non despícies.
Benígne, fac, Dómine, in bona voluntáte tua Sion: ut ædificéntur muri Jerúsalem.
Tunc acceptabis sacrificium justitiæ, oblationes, et holocausta: tunc imponent super altare tuum vitulos.

Gloria Patri, etc.

Dr. Ker, writing on the same theme in "The Psalms in History," says: "It was sung by George Wishart and his friends the night he was taken prisoner, to be afterwards burned. It was read to Lady Jane Grey and her husband, Guildford Dudley, when they were executed together, August 22, 1553—read to her in Latin, and repeated by her in English. It was also read at Norfolk's execution a few years later. For a long period in the Middle Ages, and after the Reformation, it was the Miserere, the last cry for mercy sung or heard by those who were about to step into the presence of the Judge. Most of the Huguenots made it their death-song."

## 30—GOOD FRIDAY. STABAT MATER.

This most pathetic hymn of the Middle Ages is not so well known among Protestants as it ought to be. "The vividness with which it pictures the weeping mother at the Cross, its tenderness, its beauty of rhythm, its melodious double rhymes, and its impressiveness when sung either to the fine plain song melody or in the noble compositions which many of the great masters of music have set to it, go far to justify the place it has long held in the Roman Catholic Church."

It dates in its present form from about 1150. It has been attributed to four Popes, to St. Bernard, and others, but was really written by Jacopone, Jacobus de Benedictis. The Flagellants used it to help them to bear the lashes which they inflicted on each other as they wandered from town to town in the fourteenth century. It has been translated seventy-eight times into German, and many times into every other language. It has been set to music by Palestrina, Pergolesi, Haydn, Rossini, and Dvorak. It has been Protestantised by mutilation in Hymns Ancient and Modern. I give here the Latin and English versions from the Roman Catholic Parochial Hymn-Book.

AT the cross her station keeping,
   Stood the mournful mother weeping
Close to Jesus to the last;
Through her heart His sorrow sharing,
All His bitter anguish bearing,
   Now at length the sword had passed.

Oh, how sad and sore distressed
Was that Mother highly blessed
   Of the sole-begotten One!
Christ above in torment hangs,
She beneath beholds the pangs
   Of her dying glorious Son.

Is there one who would not weep,
Whelmed in miseries so deep,
   Christ's dear Mother to behold?
Can the human heart refrain
From partaking in her pain,
   In that Mother's pain untold?

Bruised, derided, cursed, defiled,
She beheld her tender child
   All with bloody scourges rent,

For the sins of His own nation,
Saw Him hang in desolation,
   Till His spirit forth He sent.

O thou Mother! fount of love!
Touch my spirit from above,
   Make my heart with thine accord;
Make me feel as thou hast felt;
Make my soul to glow and melt
   With the love of Christ my Lord.

Holy Mother! pierce me through;
In my heart each wound renew
   Of my Saviour crucified:
Let me share with thee His pain,
Who for all my sins was slain,
   Who for me in torments died.

Let me mingle tears with thee,
Mourning Him who mourned for me.
   All the days that I may live:
By the cross with thee to stay,
There with thee to weep and pray,
   Is all I ask of thee to give.

Virgin of all virgins best,
Listen to my fond request:
   Let me share thy grief divine;
Let me, to my latest breath,
In my body bear the death
   Of that dying Son of thine.

Wounded with His every wound,
Steep my soul till it hath swooned
   In His very blood away:
Be to me, O Virgin, nigh,
Lest in flames I burn and die
   In His awful judgment day.

Christ, when thou shalt call me hence,
Be Thy Mother my defence,
  Be Thy cross my victory;
While my body here decays,
May my soul Thy goodness praise,
  Safe in Paradise with Thee.     Amen.

STABAT Mater dolorosa
    Juxta crucem lacrymosa,
  Dum pendebat Filius,
Cujus animam gementem,
Contristatam, et dolentem,
  Pertransivit gladius.

O quam tristis et afflicta
Fuit illa benedicta
  Mater Unigeniti.
Quæ mœrebat, et dolebat,
Pia Mater, dum videbat
  Nati pœnas inclyti.

Quis est homo qui non fleret,
Matrem Christi si videret
  In tanto supplicio?
Quis non posset contristari,
Christi Matrem contemplari
  Dolentem cum Filio?

Pro peccatis suæ gentis
Vidit Jesum in tormentis,
  Et flagellis subditum.
Vidit suum dulcem Natum
Moriendo desolatum,
  Dum emisit spiritum.

Eia Mater, fons amoris,
Me sentire vim doloris,
  Fac, ut tecum lugeam.

Fac ut ardeat cor meum
In amando Christum Deum,
  Ut sibi complaceam.

Sancta Mater, istud agas,
Crucifixi fige plagas
  Cordi meo valide.
Tui Nati vulnerati,
Tam dignati pro me pati,
  Pœnas mecum divide.

Fac me tecum pie flere,
Crucifixo condolere,
  Donec ego vixero.
Juxta Crucem tecum stare,
Et me tibi sociare
  In planctu desidero.

Virgo virginum præclara,
Mihi jam non sis amara;
  Fac me tecum plangere.
Fac ut portem Christi mortem,
Passionis fac consortem,
  Et plagas recolere.

Fac me plagis vulnerari.
Fac me Cruce inebriari,
  Et cruore Filii,
Flammis ne urar succensus,
Per te, Virgo, sim defensus
  In die judicii.

Christe, cum sit hinc exire
Da per Matrem me venire
  Ad palmam victoriæ.
Quando corpus morietur,
Fac ut animæ donetur
  Paradisi gloria.      Amen.

TUNE—"STABAT MATER."

When Sir Walter Scott lay dying, Lockhart, his son-in-law, after saying that they could hear him muttering some of the magnificent hymns of the Roman ritual, in which he had always delighted, adds: "We very often heard distinctly the cadence of the 'Dies Iræ,' and I think the very last stanza that we could make out was the first of a still greater favourite, 'Stabat Mater Dolorosa.'"

It is worthy of note that this poem, which holds all but the highest place in the hymnody of the Catholic Church, was composed by a man who, for his zeal for reform, was thrown into jail by the ecclesiastical authorities of his day. He lay in the dungeon to which he had been consigned until the death of Pope Boniface the Eighth, when he was released.

## 31 — EASTER. CHRIST THE LORD IS RISEN TO-DAY.

This hymn by Charles Wesley, set to Handel's "See the Conquering Hero Comes," has long been accepted as the best English Easter hymn. Yet it is curious to note that John Wesley dropped it out of the Wesleyan Hymn-Book in 1780, and it did not regain its place there till 1830.

CHRIST, the Lord, is risen to-day,
   Sons of men, and angels, say:
Raise your songs and triumphs high:
Sing, ye heavens, and earth reply.

Love's redeeming work is done:
Fought the fight, the battle won.
Lo! our sun's eclipse is o'er:
Lo! He sets in blood no more.

Vain the stone, the watch, the seal,
Christ hath burst the gates of hell;
Death, in vain, forbids Him rise;
Christ hath opened Paradise.

Lives again our glorious King;
Where, O Death, is now thy sting?
Once He died our souls to save;
Where's thy victory, O Grave?

Soar we now where Christ hath led,
Following our exalted Head:
Made like Him, like Him we rise:
Ours the cross, the grave, the skies.

Hail! the Lord of earth and heaven:
Praise to Thee by both be given,
Thee we greet triumphant now:
Hail! the Resurrection, Thou!

King of glory, soul of bliss,
Everlasting life is this,
Thee to know, Thy power to prove,
Thus to sing, and thus to love.

TUNE—"EASTER HYMN" (with Alleluias) FROM THE "LYRA DAVIDICA."

## 32—THOMAS AQUINAS'S HYMN.

A CATHOLIC friend to whom I referred the question as to the choice of hymns that have helped Catholics, insisted that I ought to include two hymns of Thomas Aquinas. The worst of Catholic hymns is that they have always to be given both in Latin and in English; therefore, instead of two by Aquinas, I only give one.

SING, my tongue, the Saviour's glory,
  Of His flesh the mystery sing;
Of the blood, all price exceeding,
Shed by our Immortal King,
Destined for the world's redemption,
From a noble womb to spring.

Of a pure and spotless Virgin
Born for us on earth below,
He, as Man with man conversing,
Stayed the seeds of truth to sow;
Then He closed in solemn order
Wondrously His life of woe.

On the night of that Last Supper,
Seated with His chosen band,
He the paschal victim eating,
First fulfils the Law's command;
Then, as food to all His brethren,
Gives Himself with His own hand.

Word made flesh, the bread of nature
By His Word to Flesh He turns;
Wine into His Blood He changes:—
What though sense no change discerns,
Only be the heart in earnest,
Faith her lesson quickly learns.

Down in adoration falling,
Lo! the Sacred Host we hail:
Lo! o'er ancient forms departing,
Newer rites of grace prevail:
Faith for all defects supplying,
Where the feeble senses fail.

To the Everlasting Father,
And the Son who reigns on high,
With the Holy Ghost proceeding
Forth from each eternally,
Be salvation, honour, blessing,
Might and endless majesty.   Amen.

PANGE lingua gloriósi
 Corporis mystérium,
Sanguinisque pretiósi,

Quem in mundi pretium
Fructus ventris generósi
Rex effudit gentium.

Nobis datus, nobis nátus
Ex intacta Vírgine,
Et in mundo conversátus,
Sparso verbi sémine,
Sui moras incolátus,
Miro clausit ordine.

In suprémæ nocte cœnæ,
Recumbens cum frátribus,
Observata lege plene
Cibis in legálibus,
Cibum turbæ duodénæ
Se dat suis manibus.

Verbum cáro panem vérum
Verbo carnem efficit:
Fitque sanguis Christi merum:
Et si sensus déficit,
Ad firmandum cor sincérum
Sola fides sufficit.

Tantum ergo Sácramentum
Venerémur cernui:
Et antíquum documentum
Novo cedat ritui:
Præstet fides supplementum
Sensuum defectui.

Genitóri, Genitóque
Laus et Jubilátio,
Salus, honor, virtus quoque
Sit et benedictio:
Procedenti ab utróque
Compar sit laudátio.   Amen.

TUNE — "PANGE LINGUA" (Ancient Plain Song).

## 33—IN COMMEMORATION OF THE DEAD.
## DE PROFUNDIS.

THE One Hundred and Thirtieth Psalm, used by the Roman Catholics on going and returning from funerals, is declared by Jeremy Taylor to be the Psalm of Psalms for the sick. It was the last psalm of Mary Queen of Scots, and was quoted at the last by the judicious Richard Hooker. It was the peculiar delight of Luther, whose version *Aus tiefer noth schrei ich zu Dir* was only less popular than his "Ein' feste Burg." It was sung at his funeral, and many a time it rallied him and his followers in the midst of despair. It was the singing of this psalm at St. Paul's that paved the way for the conversion of John Wesley.

OUT of the depths have I cried unto Thee, O Lord.

Lord, hear my voice; let Thine ears be attentive to the voice of my supplications.

If Thou, Lord, shouldest mark iniquities, O Lord, who shall stand?

But there is forgiveness with Thee, that Thou mayest be feared.

I wait for the Lord, my soul doth wait, and in His word do I hope.

My soul waiteth for the Lord more than they that watch for the morning; I say more than they that watch for the morning.

Let Israel hope in the Lord; for with the Lord there is mercy, and with Him is plenteous redemption.

And He shall redeem Israel from all His iniquities.

DE profundis clamavi ad te, Domine: Domine, exaudi vocem meam.

Fiant aures tuæ intendentes in vocem deprecationis meæ.

Si iniquitates observaveris, Domine: Domine, quis sustinebit?
Quia apud te propitiatio est: et propter legem tuam sustinuite, Domine.
Sustinuit anima mea in verbo ejus: speravit anima mea in Domino.
A custodia matutina usque ad noctem: speret Israel in Domino.
Quia apud Dominum misericordia: et copiosa apud eum redemptio.
Et ipse redimet Israel, ex omnibus iniquitatibus ejus.
 *V.*  Requiem æternam dona eis Domine.
 *R.*  Et lux perpetua luceat eis.
 *V.*  Requiescant in pace.
 *R.*  Amen.

## 34—THE DAY OF JUDGMENT.
## DIES IRAE.

THIS most famous and awful of all the hymns of the Church is supposed to have been written in the thirteenth century by Thomas of Celano, the friend and biographer of St. Francis of Assisi. Originally used as an advent hymn, it is now used as the sequence in the mass for the dead. Goethe uses it in "Faust." Sir Walter Scott, who muttered it on his death-bed, translated part of it in "The Lay of the Last Minstrel." There are said to be one hundred and sixty translations into English and ninety into German. Archbishop Trench says: "It holds a foremost place among the masterpieces of sacred song." I quote Sir Walter Scott's translation, of which Mr. Gladstone says: "I know nothing so sublime in any portion of the sacred poetry of modern times."

THAT day of wrath, that dreadful day,
 When heaven and earth shall pass away,
What power shall be the sinner's stay?
How shall he meet that dreadful day?

When, shriveling like a parched scroll,
The flaming heavens together roll;
When louder yet, and yet more dread,
Swells the high trump that wakes the dead:

Oh! on that day, that wrathful day,
When man to judgment wakes from clay,
Be Thou the trembling sinner's stay,
Though heaven and earth shall pass away!

Sir Walter did not carry his translation further.

Dr. Irons' translation was prompted by the effect produced by the singing of "Dies Iræ," when the heart of the Archbishop of Paris, who had been killed on the barricades in 1848, was displayed in the choir of Notre Dame.

DAY of wrath! O day of mourning!
See fulfilled the prophet's warning!
Heaven and earth in ashes burning.

O what fear man's bosom rendeth!
When from heaven the Judge descendeth,
On whose sentence all dependeth!

Wondrous sound the trumpet flingeth,
Through earth's sepulchres it ringeth,
All before the throne it bringeth.

Death is struck, and nature quaking,
All creation is awaking,
To its Judge an answer making.

Lo, the Book, exactly worded,
Wherein all hath been recorded!
**Thence shall judgment be awarded.**

When the Judge His seat attaineth,
And each hidden deed arraigneth,
Nothing unavenged remaineth.

What shall I, frail man, be pleading,
Who for me be interceding,
When the just are mercy needing?

King of majesty tremendous,
Who dost free salvation send us,
Fount of pity, then befriend us!

Think, good Jesus, my salvation
Caused Thy wondrous incarnation;
Leave me not to reprobation.

Faint and weary Thou hast sought me,
On the cross of suffering bought me;
Shall such grace be vainly brought me?

Righteous Judge! for sin's pollution
Grant Thy gift of absolution,
Ere that day of retribution.

Guilty, now I pour my moaning,
All my shame with anguish owning;
Spare, O God, Thy suppliant groaning!

Thou the sinful woman savedst;
Thou the dying thief forgavest;
And to me a hope vouchsafest.

Worthless are my prayers and sighing,
Yet, good Lord, in grace complying,
Rescue me from fires undying.

With Thy favoured sheep O place me,
Nor among the goats abase me;
But to Thy right hand upraise me.

While the wicked are confounded,
Doomed to flames of woe unbounded,
Call me with Thy saints surrounded.

Low I kneel, with heart submission:
See, like ashes, my contrition;
Help me in my last condition.

Ah, that day of tears and mourning!
From the dust of earth returning,
Man for judgment must prepare him;

Spare, O God, in mercy spare him!
Lord all-pitying, Jesus blest,
Grant them Thine eternal rest!

DIES iræ, dies illa
   Solvet sæclum in favilla;
Teste David cum Sybilla.

Quantus tremor est futurus
Quando Judex est venturus,
Cuncta stricte discussurus!

Tuba mirum spargens sonum
Per sepulchra regionum,
Coget omnes ante thronum.

Mors stupebit et natura,
Cum resurget creatura,
Judicanti responsura.

Liber scriptus proferetur,
In quo totum continetur,
Unde mundus judicetur.

Judex ergo cum sedebit,
Quidquid latet, apparebit:
Nil inultum remanebit.

Quid sum miser tunc dicturus?
Quem patronum rogaturus?
Cum vix justus sit securus.

Rex tremendæ majestatis,
Qui salvandos salvas gratis,
Salve me, fons pietatis.

Recordare, Jesu pie,
Quod sum causa tuæ viæ ;
Ne me perdas illa die.

Quærens me sedisti lassus,
Redemisti crucem passus ;
Tantus labor non sit cassus.

Juste Judex ultionis,
Donum fac remissionis
Ante diem rationis.

Ingemisco tanquam reus,
Culpa rubet vultus meus,
Supplicanti parce Deus.

Qui Mariam absolvisti,
Et latronem exaudisti,
Mihi quoque spem dedisti.

Preces meæ non sunt dignæ,
Sed tu bonus fac benigne,
Ne perenni cremer igne.

Inter oves locum præsta,
Et ab hœdis me sequestra.
Statuens in parte dextra.

Confutatis maledictis,
Flammis acribus addictis,
Voca me cum benedictis.

Oro supplex et acclinis,
Cor contritum quasi cinis :
Gere curam mei finis.

> Lacrymosa dies illa,
> Qua resurget ex favilla.
> Judicandus homo reus,
> Huic ergo parce Deus.
>
> Pie Jesu Domine,
> Dona eis requiem.
>     TUNE — DR. DYKES'S "DIES IRÆ."

## 35 — LO! HE COMES.

THE English hymn that supplies in the Protestant world the place of the "Dies Iræ," is the composite hymn written by Cennick and C. Wesley.

LO! He comes with clouds descending,
  Once for favoured sinners slain;
Thousand thousand saints attending
  Swell the triumph of His train:
    Hallelujah!
Jesus comes, and comes to reign.

Every eye shall then behold Him,
  Robed in dreadful majesty;
Those who set at nought and sold Him,
  Pierced and nailed Him to the tree,
    Deeply wailing,
Shall the true Messiah see.

Every island, sea, and mountain,
  Heaven and earth shall flee away:
All who hate Him must, confounded,
  Hear the summons of that day:—
    Come to judgment,
Come to judgment, come away!

Now redemption, long expected,
  See, in solemn pomp, appear;
All His saints, by man rejected,

Now shall meet Him in the air:
  Hallelujah!
See the day of God appear.

Yea, Amen; let all adore Thee,
  High on Thine eternal throne:
Saviour, take the power and glory,
  Make Thy righteous sentence known.
    O come quickly,
  Claim the kingdom for Thine own.

TUNE — "HELMSLEY," OR "ST. THOMAS."

There are many forms of this hymn, but the above is as popular as any other.

## V. — Litanies.

### 36 — WHEN OUR HEADS ARE BOWED WITH WOE.

DEAN MILMAN'S poem, on Christ's sympathy for human sorrows, was written for the sixteenth Sunday after Trinity. It is based upon the narrative (in the Gospel for that day) of Christ's miracle at Nain. As a Litany, in Lent, and at burials, the hymn is largely used. The refrain was originally written, "Gracious Son of Mary, hear!"

WHEN our heads are bowed with woe,
  When our bitter tears o'erflow,
When we mourn the lost, the dear,
Jesu, Son of Mary, hear!

Thou our throbbing flesh hast worn,
Thou our mortal griefs hast borne,
Thou hast shed the human tear;
Jesu, Son of Mary, hear!

When the solemn death-bell tolls
For our own departing souls,
When our final doom is near,
Jesu, Son of Mary, hear!

Thou hast bowed the dying head,
Thou the blood of life hast shed,
Thou hast filled a mortal bier;
Jesu, Son of Mary, hear!

When the heart is sad within
With the thought of all its sin;
When the spirit shrinks with fear;
Jesu, Son of Mary, hear!

Thou the shame, the grief, hast known —
Though the sins were not Thine own,
Thou hast deigned their load to bear;
Jesu, Son of Mary, hear!

TUNE — "REDHEAD, No. 47."

## 37 — SAVIOUR, WHEN IN DUST TO THEE.

THIS hymn, written by Sir Robert Grant, at one time Governor of Bombay under the East India Company, has received the hall-mark of helpful usefulness in all parts of the English-speaking world.

SAVIOUR, when in dust to Thee
  Low we bow the adoring knee;
When, repentant, to the skies
Scarce we lift our weeping eyes;
O! by all Thy pains and woe,
Suffered once for man below,
Bending from Thy throne on high,
Hear our solemn litany.

By Thy helpless infant years,
By Thy life of want and tears,
By Thy days of sore distress
In the savage wilderness,
By the dread mysterious hour
Of the insulting tempter's power;
Turn, O turn a favouring eye,
Hear our solemn litany.

By the sacred grief that wept
O'er the grave where Lazarus slept;
By the boding tears that flowed
Over Salem's loved abode;
By the anguished sigh that told
Treachery lurked within Thy fold;
From Thy seat above the sky,
Hear our solemn litany.

By Thine hour of dire despair,
By Thine agony of prayer;
By the cross, the nail, the thorn,
Piercing spear and torturing scorn;
By the gloom that veiled the skies
O'er the dreadful sacrifice,
Listen to our humble cry,
Hear our solemn litany.

By Thy deep expiring groan;
By the sad sepulchral stone;
By the vault whose dark abode
Held in vain the rising God;
O! from earth to heaven restored,
Mighty re-ascended Lord,
Listen, listen to the cry
Of our solemn litany.

TUNE — "MISERERE" OR "TICHFIELD."

## 38 — WHEN THE WEARY, SEEKING REST.

This Litany, by Horatius Bonar, is modelled upon the prayer of Solomon at the dedication of the Temple.

>   WHEN the weary, seeking rest,
>     To thy goodness flee;
>   When the heavy-laden cast
>     All their load on thee;
>   When the troubled, seeking peace,
>     On thy Name shall call;
>   When the sinner, seeking life,
>     At thy feet shall fall:
>  Hear then in love, O Lord, the cry,
>  In heaven thy dwelling-place on high.
>
>   When the worldling, sick at heart,
>     Lifts his soul above;
>   When the prodigal looks back
>     To his Father's love:
>   When the proud man, in his pride,
>     Stoops to seek thy face;
>   When the burdened brings his guilt
>     To thy throne of grace;
>  Hear then in love, O Lord, the cry,
>  In heaven thy dwelling-place on high.
>
>   When the stranger asks a home,
>     All his toils to end;
>   When the hungry craveth food,
>     And the poor a friend;
>   When the sailor on the wave
>     Bows the fervent knee;
>   When the soldier on the field
>     Lifts his heart to thee:
>  Hear then in love, O Lord, the cry,
>  In heaven thy dwelling-place on high.

When the man of toil and care
　In the city crowd ;
When the shepherd on the moor
　Names the name of God ;
When the learned and the high,
　Tired of earthly fame,
Upon higher joys intent,
　Name the blessèd Name :
Hear then in love, O Lord, the cry,
In heaven thy dwelling-place on high.

When the child, with grave fresh lip,
　Youth or maiden fair ;
When the aged, weak and grey,
　Seek thy face in prayer ;
When the widow weeps to thee,
　Sad and lone and low ;
When the orphan brings to thee
　All his orphan woe :
Hear then in love, O Lord, the cry,
In heaven thy dwelling-place on high.

　　　　　　　　Tune — "Intercession."

Bishop Fraser of Manchester used to say that he regarded this as the finest hymn in the English language. His second favourite was "I heard the voice of Jesus say."

## VI. — Guidance.

### 39 — LEAD, KINDLY LIGHT.

Of all the modern hymns praying for guidance, Newman's famous three verses seem to be most popular, — especially with people who have not accepted the leading of any church or theological authority. "The only hymn of which words and music touched any chord in me," wrote the Hon. Reginald Brett, "is Cardinal Newman's 'Lead, Kindly Light.' My opinion is that the music and the congregational singing are the causes of emotion, not the words of any hymn." Cardinal Newman seems to have been very much of the same opinion. He once remarked that he was deeply thankful for the hold his hymn had obtained on the public; but, he added, "it is not the hymn but the tune that has gained the popularity." This is undoubtedly true in certain quarters. In the séance rooms of Chicago it was constantly sung while the medium was waiting for materialization or other manifestations, chiefly on account of the tune and the reference in the last verse to "angel faces." But, on the other hand, the hymn has the first place in the favour of such fervent Catholics as the Marquis of Ripon and Mr. Justin McCarthy, and such stout Protestants as Sir Evelyn Wood and a leading member of Lord Rosebery's Cabinet. Mrs. Lynn Linton (who may be said to represent the Agnostics) and Mr. Thomas Hardy include it among their three first favourites. The hymn was not at first included in some Nonconformist hymnals. Mr. Richard Le Gallienne, the poet, for instance, writes: "I was brought up among the Baptists, who, if I remember aright, did not in my time sing, 'Lead, Kindly Light,' which I learned to love in a late period of church-going. That seems to me," he adds, "if one had to choose, the finest of all hymns, as it contains piety and poetry in the highest proportion." The Rev. Dr. Rigg, who may be regarded as the best representative of the old school of Wesleyans, writes as follows about the hymn:—

"'Lead, Kindly Light,' is a great favourite with very many, being a hymn that touches the heart and expresses, more or less, the experience of many souls. Certainly it is one which might often have expressed, more or less distinctly, my own experience; but I have not found it a helpful hymn for deliverance, or a strengthening hymn in distress and conflict. It conduces to resignation, it may be, but scarcely leads on to victory. It is not in our Methodist collection, and I could not say that it has been a helpful hymn to me spiritually, though it is a touching poem, and in various ways prophetic of the experience of its writer."

No doubt it is somewhat hard for the staunch Protestant to wax enthusiastic over the invocation of a "Kindly Light" which led its author straight into the arms of the Scarlet Woman of the Seven Hills. Against this may be put the fact that when the Parliament of Religions met at Chicago, the representatives of every creed known to man found two things on which they were agreed. They could all join in the Lord's Prayer, and they could all sing, "Lead, Kindly Light." This hymn, Mrs. Drew tells me, and "Rock of Ages," are two of Mr. Gladstone's "most favourite hymns."

LEAD, kindly Light, amid the encircling gloom;
    Lead thou me on:
The night is dark, and I am far from home;
    Lead thou me on.
Keep thou my feet; I do not ask to see
The distant scene; one step enough for me.

I was not ever thus, nor prayed that thou
    Should'st lead me on:
I loved to choose and see my path; but now,
    Lead thou me on.
I loved the garish day, and, spite of fears,
Pride ruled my will; remember not past years.

So long thy power hath blest me, sure it still
    Will lead me on,
O'er moor and fen, o'er crag and torrent, till
    The night is gone,
And with the morn those angel faces smile,
Which I have loved long since, and lost awhile.

            TUNE — "LUX BENIGNA."

"It seems to me rather singular," writes a correspondent in Wales, "that verses so full of faith as 'Lead,

Kindly Light,' should be mentioned with such approval by so many sceptics." He then sends me the following attempt to express the views of an Agnostic, thoughtful, humble, and reverent, but quite unable to attain to Newman's standpoint.

The way is dark: I cry amid the gloom
      For guiding light;
A wanderer, none knows whence or what his doom,
      I brave the night.
Fair scenes afar, as in a dream, I see,
Then seem to wake, and faith deserteth me.

In wondering awe I bend the knee before
      The viewless Might;
And all my heart in mute appeal I pour,
      While straining sight
Peers o'er the waste, yet Him I cannot find
Whom seeks my soul: I grope as grope the blind.

But 'mid confusing phantom-lights I strive
      To go aright:
A still small voice leads on, and love doth give
      An inward might;
And spite of sense, their lives a silent trust
That day will dawn, that man is more than dust.

                                    R. M. L.

Another correspondent remarks: "To my mind there is only a spirit of sadness, the blind groping in the dark in loneliness and helplessness. Surely, this is not the highest hope of a follower of Christ."

On the other hand, a Scotchman writes as follows:—
"My spiritual experience has been varied. I was baptised in the Roman Catholic Church, brought up in the Congregational Independent, and at length I was fascinated by the history, energy, and enthusiasm of the Wesleyans. I was at one time a local preacher in that

body with a view to the ministry. But my fervid fit of exaltation was choked with the dusty facts of life, and smouldered down into a dry indifference. I sought nourishment in secularism and agnosticism, but found none. I was in the slough of despond, at the centre of indifference, with the everlasting 'no' on my lips, when 'Lead, kindly light, amid the encircling gloom' came to my troubled soul like the voice of angels. Wandering in the wilderness, 'o'er moor and fen, o'er crag and torrent,' Newman's Hymn was to me a green oasis, a healing spring, the shadow of a great rock. Through the light and power of God I was led to light and love in Christ in a way I had never before known or experienced."

A "Friend" writes: "If thou art sending to Mr. Stead with regard to hymns, I should put for myself rather high 'Lead, Kindly Light,' not only because of its beautiful words, but also because of him who felt them and wrote them. It is such an instruction that so great an intellect found without Christ nothing but an 'encircling gloom'—that so powerful a nature, a leader among men, wished to be 'humble as a child and guided where to go.'"

## 40—GUIDE ME, O THOU GREAT JEHOVAH.

FOR those who have been brought up on the Bible and who have never suffered the bewilderment of the Agnostic, this famous Welsh hymn in its English dress is worth a hundred "Lead, Kindly Lights." It was written at the close of last century by William Williams, a popular Calvinistic-Methodist evangelist and hymnwriter. It was Richard Knill the missionary's favourite hymn, and was constantly on his lips when dying. The last verse has been the comfort of many a dying Christian, and it has been sung and is still being sung around death-beds, to the accompaniment of heart-choking sobs and streaming tears. Here is a hymn that has helped indeed.

GUIDE me, O Thou Great Jehovah!
  Pilgrim through this barren land:
I am weak, but Thou art mighty,
  Hold me with Thy powerful hand.
    Bread of heaven!
Feed me till I want no more.

Open Thou the crystal fountain,
  Whence the healing streams do flow:
Let the fiery, cloudy pillar
  Lead me all my journey through:
    Strong Deliverer!
Be Thou still my strength and shield.

When I tread the verge of Jordan,
  Bid my anxious fears subside:
Death of death, and hell's Destruction!
  Land me safe on Canaan's side;
    Songs of praises
I will ever give to Thee.

TUNE — "DISMISSAL."

## 41 — THE LORD'S MY SHEPHERD.

If "Lead, Kindly Light," is English, and "Guide me, O Thou Great Jehovah," is Welsh, "The Lord's my Shepherd" is Scotch.

THE Lord's my shepherd, I'll not want.
  He makes me down to lie
In pastures green: he leadeth me
  the quiet waters by.

My soul he doth restore again;
  and me to walk doth make
Within the paths of righteousness,
  ev'n for his own name's sake.

Yea, though I walk in death's dark vale,
   yet will I fear none ill:
For thou art with me; and thy rod
   and staff me comfort still.

My table thou hast furnished
   in presence of my foes;
My head thou dost with oil anoint,
   and my cup overflows.

Goodness and mercy all my life
   shall surely follow me:
And in God's house for evermore
   my dwelling-place shall be.

                    TUNE—"KILMARNOCK."

"For me," writes Mr. S. R. Crockett, the popular author of the "Raiders" and many another delightful romance, "there is no hymn like 'The Lord's my Shepherd, I'll not want.' I think I must have stood by quite a hundred men and women as they lay a-dying, and I can assure you that these words—the first learned by the child—were also the words that ushered most of them out into the Quiet. To me, and to most among these Northern hills, there are no words like them."

Dr. John Ker says: "Every line of it, every word of it, has been engraven for generations on Scottish hearts, has accompanied them from childhood to age, from their homes to all the seas and lands where they have wandered, and has been to a multitude no man can number the rod and staff of which it speaks, to guide and guard them in dark valleys, and at last through the darkest." Of its helpfulness in times of crisis many instances are given, of which that which appeals most to me is the story of Marian Harvey, the servant lass of twenty, who was executed at Edinburgh with Isabel Alison for having attended the preaching of Donald Cargill, and for helping his escape. As the brave lasses were being led to the scaffold, a curate pestered them with his prayers. "Come, Isabel," said Marian, "let us sing the Twenty-third Psalm." And sing it they did, a thrilling duet on their pilgrimage to the gallows-tree. It was rough on the Covenanters in those days, and their paths did not exactly, to outward seeming, lead them by the green pastures and still waters. But they got there somehow, the Twenty-third Psalm helping them no little. This was the psalm John Ruskin first learnt at his mother's knee. It was this which Edward Irving recited at the last as he lay dying. Even poor Heinrich Heine, on his mattress-grave, in one of his latest poems, recalls the image of the Shepherd Guide whose "Pastures green and sweet refresh the wanderer's weary feet." The magnificent assurance of the fourth verse has in every age given pluck to the heart of the timid and strengthened the nerve of heroes. When St. Francis of Assisi went alone, bareheaded and barefoot, to convert the Sultan, he kept up his spirit on his solitary pilgrimage by chanting this verse. The Moslems did him no harm, and instead of taking off his head, returned him safe and sound to the pale of Christendom.

The Rev. D. P. Alford writes me: "When I was chaplain of the Scilly Islands, one of my leading parishioners, a Scotchman, when dying, found the greatest consolation in the metrical version of this psalm. His wife said to me: 'It is no wonder that psalm comforts him, for he has said it every night before going to bed ever since I have known him.' They were elderly people, and had been married many years."

In the United States the paraphrase beginning "The King of Love my Shepherd is," is the one commonly used.

## 42—JESUS, STILL LEAD ON.

AFTER the English, Welsh, and Scottish comes in due sequence the German lyrical cry for guidance, Zinzendorf's Hymn, which is said to be the first taught to the children in every German household. In German it begins,—

>Jesu, geh voran
>Auf der Lebensbahn.

The English version is as follows:—

>JESUS, still lead on
>   Till our rest be won:
>And although the way be cheerless,
>We will follow, calm and fearless:
>   Guide us by Thy hand
>   To our Fatherland.
>
>If the way be drear,
>If the foe be near,
>Let not faithless fears o'ertake us,
>Let not faith and hope forsake us;
>   For, through many a foe,
>   To our home we go.
>
>When we seek relief
>From a long-felt grief:
>When oppressed by new temptations,
>Lord, increase and perfect patience;
>   Show us that bright shore
>   Where we weep no more.
>
>Jesus, still lead on
>Till our rest be won:
>Heavenly Leader, still direct us,
>Still support, console, protect us,
>   Till we safely stand
>   In our Fatherland.

TUNE—"WESTON."

## 43—HE LEADETH ME.

THIS hymn with its chorus came to us from across the Atlantic with Mr. Sankey. It was written by Joseph H.

Gilmore, in 1859, at the close of a lecture in the First Baptist Church, Philadelphia. It has helped me many a time and oft, and I expect that it will help me now and always to the end.

HE leadeth me! Oh, blessèd thought!
Oh words with heavenly comfort fraught!
Whate'er I do, where'er I be,
Still 'tis God's hand that leadeth me.
  He leadeth me! He leadeth me!
  By His own hand He leadeth me;
  His faithful follower I would be,
  For by His hand He leadeth me.

Sometimes 'mid scenes of deepest gloom,
Sometimes where Eden's bowers bloom,
By waters calm, o'er troubled sea,
Still 'tis God's hand that leadeth me.

Lord, I would clasp Thy hand in mine;
Nor ever murmur nor repine;
Content, whatever lot I see,
Since 'tis my God that leadeth me.

And when my task on earth is done,
When, by Thy grace, the victory 's won,
E'en death's cold wave I will not flee,
Since Thou through Jordan leadest me.

       TUNE — FROM SANKEY'S "SONGS AND SOLOS."

## 44 — I DO NOT ASK, O LORD.

AMONG the most helpful hymns of modern times is Adelaide Procter's Prayer for Guidance. Like the author of "Lead, Kindly Light," Miss Procter died in the Roman Communion.

I DO not ask, O Lord, that life may be
  A pleasant road;

I do not ask that Thou wouldst take from me
    Aught of its load.

I do not ask that flowers should always spring
    Beneath my feet;
I know too well the poison and the sting
    Of things too sweet.

For one thing only, Lord, dear Lord, I plead:
    Lead me aright,
Though strength should falter and though heart should bleed,
    Through peace to light.

I do not ask, O Lord, that Thou shouldst shed
    Full radiance here;
Give but a ray of peace, that I may tread
    Without a fear.

I do not ask my cross to understand,
    My way to see;
Better in darkness just to feel Thy hand,
    And follow Thee.

Joy is like restless day; but peace divine
    Like quiet night.
Lead me, O Lord, till perfect day shall shine,
    Through peace to light.

                TUNE — BARNBY'S "AD LUCEM."

## 45—GOD MOVES IN A MYSTERIOUS WAY.

COWPER's hymn has helped multitudes to bear up under the blows of apparently adverse fortune. Within a year of the writing of this beautiful and touching hymn, Cowper's reason reeled, and he endeavoured to commit suicide by drowning in the Ouse. It is some poor consolation to know that his attempt at suicide was not a suicide of despair, but rather the perversion of the spirit of resignation and joyful submission which finds expression in the hymn. Newton says that Cowper tried to take his life, believing it was a sacrifice which God required at his hands. The accepted legend is that he had proposed to commit suicide at a certain place, but as the driver of the postchaise could not find it, he returned home without putting his purpose into execution, and there composed this hymn.

GOD moves in a mysterious way
   His wonders to perform:
He plants His footsteps in the sea,
   And rides upon the storm.

Deep in unfathomable mines
   Of never-failing skill,
He treasures up His bright designs,
   And works His sovereign will.

Ye fearful saints, fresh courage take:
   The clouds ye so much dread
Are big with mercy, and shall break
   In blessings on your head.

Judge not the Lord by feeble sense,
   But trust Him for His grace:
Behind a frowning providence
   He hides a smiling face.

His purposes will ripen fast,
   Unfolding every hour:
The bud may have a bitter taste,
   But sweet will be the flower.

Blind unbelief is sure to err,
   And scan His work in vain:
God is His own Interpreter,
   And He will make it plain.

TUNE—"ST. LEONARD'S" OR "LONDON NEW."

The third verse has been much used in times of danger and distress. It was often sung during the cotton famine, and there are few persons who cannot recall times and seasons when its comforting assurances helped to give fortitude and tranquillity to the soul. It would be difficult to find a hymn which more exactly corresponds to Lord Wolseley's ideal of a hymn, "plenty of consolation and not too much theology."

## 46 — WHEN GATHERING CLOUDS AROUND I VIEW.

THIS is another of the hymns by Sir R. Grant, at one time Governor of Bombay.

WHEN gathering clouds around I view,
And days are dark and friends are few,
On Him I lean, who not in vain
Experienced every human pain.
He sees my wants, allays my fears,
And counts and treasures up my tears.

If aught should tempt my soul to stray
From heavenly wisdom's narrow way,
To flee the good I would pursue,
Or do the sin I would not do;
Still He, who felt temptation's power,
Shall guard me in that dangerous hour.

If wounded love my bosom swell,
Deceived by those I prized too well,
He shall His pitying aid bestow,
Who felt on earth severer woe,
At once betrayed, denied, or fled,
By those who shared His daily bread.

If vexing thoughts within me rise,
And, sore dismayed, my spirit dies:
Yet He, who once vouchsafed to bear

The sickening anguish of despair,
Shall sweetly soothe, shall gently dry
The throbbing heart, the streaming eye.

When sorrowing o'er some stone I bend,
Which covers what was once a friend;
And from his hand, his voice, his smile,
Divides me for a little while,
My Saviour marks the tears I shed:
For Jesus wept o'er Lazarus dead.

And O! when I have safely passed
Through every conflict but the last:
Still, still unchanging, watch beside
My dying bed — for Thou hast died:
Then point to realms of cloudless day,
And wipe the latest tear away.

TUNE — "STELLA."

This was one of the favourites of John Gough, the great temperance lecturer.

When the late Sir Edward Baines, founder and proprietor of the *Leeds Mercury*, and veteran reformer, lay dying, he asked his family to sing this hymn, after which he said with great thankfulness: "I feel inexpressibly full of His presence and glory."

## 47 — THE LORD WILL PROVIDE.

FOR simplicity and unwavering confidence, there are few hymns of guidance to compare with this little song and chorus from Mr. Sankey's collection.

IN some way or other the Lord will provide;
  It may not be *my* way, it may not be *thy* way;
And yet in His *own* way, "the Lord will provide."
    Then we'll trust in the Lord, and He will
      provide;
    Yes, we'll trust in the Lord, and He will
      provide.

At some time or other the Lord will provide:
It may not be *my* time, it may not be *thy* time;
And yet in His *own* time, "the Lord will provide."

Despond then no longer; the Lord will provide:
And this be the token — no word He hath spoken
Was ever yet broken: "the Lord will provide."

March on then right boldly: the sea shall divide;
The pathway made glorious, with shoutings victorious,
We'll join in the chorus, "The Lord will provide."

TUNE — FROM "SONGS AND SOLOS."

## 48 — BEGONE, UNBELIEF.

THIS hymn, by John Newton, has been a wonderful stand-by to multitudes. Newton, before he became a hymn-writer, had gone the pace indeed in his youth, but had experienced one of those marvellous conversions which are the moral miracles of life. He came through much tribulation into a state in which he could write: "I commit my soul to my gracious God and Saviour, who mercifully spared me when I was an apostate, a blasphemer, and an infidel, and delivered me from that state of misery on the coast of Africa into which my obstinate wickedness had plunged me, and who has pleased to admit me (though most unworthy) to preach His glorious gospel."

BEGONE, unbelief,
  My Saviour is near,
And for my relief
  Will surely appear;
By prayer let me wrestle,
  And He will perform;
With Christ in the vessel,
  I smile at the storm.

Though dark be my way,
   Since He is my guide,
'T is mine to obey,
   'T is His to provide:
Though cisterns be broken,
   And creatures all fail,
The word He hath spoken
   Shall surely prevail.

His love, in time past,
   Forbids me to think
He 'll leave me at last
   In trouble to sink:
Each sweet Ebenezer
   I have in review,
Confirms His good pleasure
   To help me quite through.

Determined to save,
   He watched o'er my path,
When, Satan's blind slave,
   I sported with death.
And can He have taught me
   To trust in His name,
And thus far have brought me
   To put me to shame?

Why should I complain
   Of want or distress,
Temptation or pain?—
   He told me no less;
The heirs of salvation,
   I know from His Word,
Through much tribulation
   Must follow their Lord.

How bitter that cup,
   No heart can conceive,

Which He drank quite up,
  That sinners might live!
His way was much rougher
  And darker than mine;
Did Jesus thus suffer,
  And shall I repine?

Since all that I meet
  Shall work for my good,
The bitter is sweet,
  The medicine, food;
Though painful at present,
  'T will cease before long,
And then, oh, how pleasant
  The conqueror's song!

TUNE — "HANOVER."

Among the multitudinous testimonies which poured in upon me from those who had been helped by hymns, none touched me more than the story told by a poor Lancashire lass who, under the stress of passionate temptation, had forgotten the responsibilities of her position as Sunday-school teacher and the obligations of her maidenhood. She married her lover before her child was born, but the sense of her sin burnt like vitriol into her life. She wrote: "It seemed to me no soul in hell could be blacker than mine. To feel that I had disgraced the Master's service and dishonoured His Holy Name, was the bitterest drop in my cup. Never shall I forget those awful months, nay, years of torture. If any soul doubts the reality of a hell, let him live through what I lived then. I have been there, and know it exists. My girls brought me out and begged me to go back to teach. Good God! a thing like me to go back to teach these poor innocent creatures! I shrunk away, feeling I could never desecrate the threshold of God's house by my presence. They came again; it was Christmas Eve. They sang the carols at our door, and then came in, kissing and making much of me. Presently my husband began to play on the piano the dear old hymn, 'Begone, unbelief,' the girls all joining in with lips untouched by care. I had to leave the room. All the pent-up agony of months were in the strain since I was not even fit to sing it, and then kneeling at my bedside in the darkness, there came to me two lines of the hymn they had been singing:—

> How bitter that cup no heart can conceive
> Which He drank quite up that SINNERS might live.

Bitterer than even mine, I thought, and He drank it for *me*. That was the miracle for me, and I knew myself forgiven, knew that the Christ was looking at me, not with angry, but with pitying eyes. Ah, the blessedness of it! But do you suppose I could ever forgive myself more than ever I blamed and hated myself? And now there came to me a messenger direct from God. One of the friends who visited the place quarterly called to see me; when he rose to go he laid his hand on my shoulder, and, looking me straight in the face, said: 'My child, when are you going back to your work? They need you there, your class needs you, the whole school needs you, and *God* wants you. If you have done wrong, go and *atone* for it.' He left me, but his words were alive — atone for it: could I? Was that the way the Master would have me take, show Him how real my sorrow was by trying to save others from the pit into which I had fallen? If that were so, then I could brave sneers and ridicule, stand to be despised and looked down upon, if only I might in some degree atone, and show forth my loyalty and love for Him, I would do or bear whatsoever He chose, and so I went back to service to bear and endure, and be tested, and I carried with me into the fight the last verse of my hymn.

> Since all that I meet doth work for my good,
> The bitter is sweet, the medicine food.
> Though painful at present, 't will cease before long,
> And then, oh, how pleasant the conqueror's song.

"That verse was my help and stay through all the long, weary years when I slowly climbed my way back to peace and happiness, and the esteem of those whom I respected and desired should respect me. Can you wonder that this hymn is precious to me, that I hold it dearer than all others, and I think until I stand in His presence it will be one of the most hallowed and sacred of my possessions. My story is done; it is not the story of saint or martyr, but of a girl's sorrow and sin, of a woman's struggle and victory through Christ Jesus. It has not been an easy task to write it; one does n't as a rule 'volunteer heart history to a crowd,' but there are other girls in the world passing through the self-same trials, and if my life-story can help them I have no right to hold it back."

A lady writing from the Citadel of Cairo, says of this hymn: "I am surprised and disappointed to find that it is not in the *Sunday at Home* list. It is the hymn that I love best of the hundreds that I know; it has helped me scores of times in the dark days of my life, and has never failed to inspire me with fresh hope and confidence when 'life looked dark and dreary;' and it is dear to me from associations with the memory of the best of fathers. To him, in his many and sore troubles, it was a source of comfort and help, and, I believe, was to him a sort of link by which he held on to God. To me the words are not doggerel at all, they are just lovely. I often go about singing them when alone, to help me on in the way."

## 49—GIVE TO THE WINDS THY FEARS.

MR. STEVENSON, in his notes on the Methodist Hymn-Book, says: "There is not a hymn in the book which has afforded more comfort and encouragement than this to the Lord's tried people." The legend connected with this hymn recalls the delightful tales in the lives of the Saints. The origin of the hymn itself is not unworthy the record of its subsequent exploits. Gerhardt was exiled from Brandenburg by the Grand Elector in 1659. The said Grand Elector wished to "tune his pulpits." Gerhardt refused to preach save what he found in God's Word. Notice to quit thereupon being promptly served upon the intrepid preacher, he tramped forth a homeless exile, accompanied by his wife and children. Wife and weans at night, wearied and weeping, sought refuge in a wayside inn. Gerhardt, unable to comfort them, went out into the wood to pray. As he prayed, the text "Commit thy way unto the Lord, trust also in Him and He shall bring it to pass," recurred to his mind and comforted him so amazingly that he paced to and fro under the forest trees and began composing a hymn which, being Englished by John Wesley, has deservedly become a great comfort to all English-speaking peoples. Returning to the inn, he cheered his wife with his text and his hymn, and they went to bed rejoicing in confident hope that God would take care of them. They had hardly retired before a thunderous knocking at the door roused them all. It was a mounted messenger from Duke Christian of Merseburg, riding in hot haste to deliver a sealed packet to Dr. Gerhardt. The good doctor opened it, and read therein a hearty invitation from the Duke, who offered him "church, people, home, and livelihood, and liberty to preach the Gospel as your heart may prompt you." So, adds the chronicle, the Lord took care of His servant. Here is a portion of the hymn which was composed under such singular circumstances.

GIVE to the winds thy fears;
   Hope, and be undismayed:
God hears thy sighs, and counts thy tears:
   God shall lift up thy head.
   Through waves, through clouds and storms,
     He gently clears the way.
Wait thou His time; so shall the night
   Soon end in joyous day.

He everywhere hath sway,
  And all things serve His might;
His every act pure blessing is,
  His path unsullied light.
When He makes bare His arm,
  What shall His work withstand?
When He His people's cause defends,
  Who, who shall stay His hand?

Leave to His sovereign will
  To choose, and to command;
With wonder filled, thou then shalt own
  How wise, how strong His hand.
Thou comprehend'st Him not;
  Yet earth and heaven tell,
God sits as Sovereign on the throne;
  He ruleth all things well.

Thou seest our weakness, Lord;
  Our hearts are known to Thee.
O lift Thou up the sinking hand;
  Confirm the feeble knee.
Let us, in life and death,
  Boldly Thy truth declare;
And publish, with our latest breath,
  Thy love and guardian care.

          Tune — Dr. Gauntlett's "St. George."

There is a long list of worthies who have been cheered in life and death by this hymn, but the champion story of them all is the Legend of the Raven. I must quote it intact: —

In a village near Warsaw there lived a pious German peasant named Dobyr. Without remedy he had fallen into arrears of rent, and his landlord threatened to evict him. It was winter. Thrice he appealed for a respite, but in vain. It was evening, and the next day his family were to be turned out into the snow. Dobyr kneeled down in the midst of his family. After prayer they sang:—

> Commit thou all thy griefs
> And ways into His hands.

As they came to the last verse, in German, of Part I.,

> When Thou wouldst all our need supply,
> Who, who shall stay Thy hand?

there was a knock at the window close by where he knelt, and opening it Dobyr was met by a raven, one which his grandfather had tamed and set at liberty. In its bill was a ring, set with precious stones. This he took to his minister, who said at once that it belonged to the King Stanislaus, to whom he returned it, and related his story. The King sent for Dobyr, and besides rewarding him on the spot, built for him, next year, a new house, and stocked his cattle stalls from the royal domain. Over the house door, on an iron tablet, there is carved a raven with a ring in its beak, and underneath this address to Divine Providence:—

> Thou everywhere hast sway,
> And all things serve Thy might;
> Thy every act pure blessing is,
> Thy path unsullied light.

## 50—FATHER, I KNOW THAT ALL MY LIFE.

Miss Waring, like Charlotte Elliott and Adelaide Procter, made notable contributions to the hymnody of Resignation. This hymn of Miss Waring's has helped myriads.

> FATHER, I know that all my life
>     Is portioned out for me,
> The changes that will surely come,
>     I do not fear to see;

I ask Thee for a present mind
   Intent on pleasing Thee.

I ask Thee for a thoughtful love,
   Through constant watching wise,
To meet the glad with joyful smiles,
   And wipe the weeping eyes;
A heart at leisure from itself,
   To soothe and sympathise.

I would not have the restless will
   That hurries to and fro,
That seeks for some great thing to do,
   Or secret thing to know;
I would be treated as a child,
   And guided where I go.

Wherever in the world I am,
   In whatsoe'er estate,
I have a fellowship with hearts
   To keep and cultivate;
A work of lowly love to do
   For Him on whom I wait.

I ask Thee for the daily strength,
   To none that ask denied;
A mind to blend with outward life,
   While keeping at Thy side:
Content to fill a little space,
   If Thou be glorified.

Briers beset our every path,
   Which call for patient care;
There is a cross in every lot,
   A constant need for prayer:
But lowly hearts that lean on Thee
   Are happy everywhere.

In service which Thy love appoints,
  There are no bonds for me.
My secret heart is taught the truth
  That makes Thy children free:
A life of self-renouncing love
  Is one of liberty.

          TUNE — "LEBANON," FROM SPOHR.

A clergyman who has at last been compelled by the loss of his voice to abandon his living, writes me as follows: —

"This hymn has been a more definite help in stimulating the heart to considerate kindness and cheerful trust. A year ago my voice failed me, and the spring of 1895 found me seeking recovery in rest and change of air; but haunted with the fear that this loss of voice might be permanent, and that I might have to resign my living and give up my life's work, whilst yet almost in the vigour of life. This fear was verified, and I resigned my living last July. But, as usually happens, the actual trial was not so depressing as the fear of it."

A lady in the West of England sends me this note on this hymn, and how it helped her: —

"This hymn was sung one Sunday when I had wandered into a strange place of worship — a Wesleyan chapel, I think. I was simply eaten up with ambition and the craving to know the secret things, and do the great ones of Life; and this hymn showed me The Better Way. I saw that it was good to be content, 'to fill a little space,' and in a sort of waking vision I saw that great things were not for me, but as someone (Dante, perhaps) has said: 'In God's will lies our place.' So you see my hymn was the overture to my little Act of Renunciation, and now I black stoves and dust rooms, and possess my soul in patience, and understand *a little* what the 'Peace that passeth understanding' may mean."

Another lady writes me: "This hymn came to me

when I was a girl of eighteen, and it has continued its power over me till now, over twenty years. It seems to me that ideal Christian service, for women, at all events, is 'a heart at leisure from itself to soothe and sympathise.' Many times these lines, turned into a prayer, have led me to get the better of the demon of selfishness."

## 51—THE 121st PSALM.

MR. CROCKETT places this psalm second only to the Twenty-third. It was one of the two psalms—the One Hundred and Thirty-fifth being the other—that David Livingstone read on the morning of the day when he first quitted Scotland for the African mission-field. It was known as the Traveller's Psalm from the days of Bishop Hooper, who used it before setting out on a journey.

I TO the hills will lift mine eyes,
   from whence doth come mine aid.

My safety cometh from the Lord,
   who heav'n and earth hath made.

Thy foot he'll not let slide, nor will
   he slumber that thee keeps.

Behold, he that keeps Israel,
   he slumbers not, nor sleeps.

The Lord thee keeps, the Lord thy shade
   on thy right hand doth stay:

The moon by night thee shall not smite,
   nor yet the sun by day.

The Lord shall keep thy soul; he shall
   preserve thee from all ill.

Henceforth thy going out and in
   God keep for ever will.

TUNE—"SOLOMON," FROM HANDEL.

Mr. Marson notes that Edward, the Black Prince, chose the first clause of the second verse as the motto for the coins struck in England in 1362. In the United States Tate & Brady's paraphrase, beginning, "To Sion's Hill I lift my eyes," is the popular version.

## VII.—Resignation.

### 52—LORD, IT BELONGS NOT TO MY CARE.

RICHARD BAXTER, the author of the "Saints' Everlasting Rest," had a tolerably troubled time—without much rest in it—on this side the grave. He was troubled by the Independents under Cromwell; by the Royalists after the Restoration, who ejected him; and by Judge Jeffreys, who bullied and abused him. But these were only of the outside and of the surface; within, the old saint had an everlasting rest of his own. The secret of this peace he expressed in the following hymn:—

LORD, it belongs not to my care,
    Whether I die or live;
To love and serve Thee is my share,
    And this Thy grace must give.

If life be long I will be glad,
    That I may long obey;
If short—yet why should I be sad
    To soar to endless day?

Christ leads me through no darker rooms
    Than He went through before;
He that into God's kingdom comes,
    Must enter by His door.

Come, Lord, when grace hath made me meet
    Thy blessed face to see;
For if Thy work on earth be sweet,
    What will Thy glory be?

Then I shall end my sad complaints
  And weary sinful days;
And join with the triumphant saints
  To sing Jehovah's praise.

My knowledge of that life is small,
  The eye of faith is dim;
But 't is enough that Christ knows all,
  And I shall be with Him.

TUNE — "ARISTIDES."

An old widow writes: "The hymn that has the sweetest and tenderest memories for me is that of Baxter's. I repeated it in my last farewell words to my husband, and he echoed it with his dying lips, and then said: 'It is enough that Christ knows all, and that I shall be with Him.'" A missionary writes to me from Wenchow describing how one verse in this hymn helped him. When a student in Manchester his spirit shrunk from the sacrifice entailed by dedication to the work of a missionary in China. He was convinced that he could not stand the climate, and that he would very shortly die if he went out to the Far East. "One day as I was kneeling in prayer in my room at the College, I was more miserable in spirit than usual, when, like a heaven-sent message, the first three verses of Richard Baxter's beautiful hymn came to me. The first verse is, as you know, as follows: —

    'Lord, it belongs not to my care,
      Whether I die or live;
    To love and serve Thee is my share,
      And this Thy grace must give.'

Light, liberty, and strength came with the message of this hymn, which at the time became the words of my prayer, instead of the doubting and hesitating thoughts of my heart. For four years I have been working in this land of China, and the message of Baxter's hymn still abides with me as a source of comfort and strength."

## 53—O LORD, HOW HAPPY SHOULD WE BE.

JOSEPH ANSTICE, Professor of Classical Literature at King's College, London, who died in 1836, at the age of twenty-eight, wrote the following hymn, with others, during his last illness:—

O LORD, how happy should we be,
   If we could cast our care on Thee;
If we from self could rest,
And feel, at heart, that One above,
In perfect wisdom, perfect love,
   Is working for the best:

Could we but kneel and cast our load,
E'en while we pray, upon our God;
   Then rise with lightened cheer,
Sure that the Father, who is nigh
To still the famished raven's cry,
   Will hear in that we fear.

How far from this, our daily life!
Ever disturbed by anxious strife,
   By sudden, wild alarms:
O could we but relinquish all
Our earthly props, and simply fall
   On Thine almighty arms!

TUNE — "INNSBRUCK."

## 54—THY WAY, NOT MINE, O LORD.

THE Scotch Presbyterian, Dr. Bonar, joins in with this familiar hymn:—

THY way, not mine, O Lord,
   However dark it be;
Lead me by Thine own hand,
   Choose out the path for me.

Smooth let it be or rough,
  It will be still the best;
Winding or straight, it leads
  Right onward to Thy rest.

I dare not choose my lot;
  I would not if I might:
Choose Thou for me, my God,
  So shall I walk aright.

The kingdom that I seek
  Is Thine: so let the way
That leads to it be Thine,
  Else I must surely stray.

Take Thou my cup, and it
  With joy or sorrow fill,
As best to Thee may seem;
  Choose Thou my good and ill.

Choose Thou for me my friends,
  My sickness or my health;
Choose Thou my cares for me,
  My poverty or wealth.

        TUNE—"ST. DENYS" OR "FIDUCIA."

## 55—'TIS MY HAPPINESS BELOW.

COWPER, who had more than the ordinary share of the burdens of life, made the best of his sad case in this hymn, which has dispelled more gloom than ever Cowper suffered.

'TIS my happiness below,
  Not to live without the cross,
But the Saviour's power to know,
Sanctifying every loss.

Trials must and will befall:
But with humble faith to see

Love inscribed upon them all,
This is happiness to me.

God, in Israel, sows the seeds
Of affliction, pain, and toil;
These spring up and choke the weeds
Which would else o'erspread the soil.

Trials make the promise sweet;
Trials give new life to prayer;
Trials bring me to His feet,
Lay me low and keep me there.

Did I meet no trials here,
No correction by the way,
Might I not with reason fear
I should prove a cast-away?

Worldlings may escape the rod,
Sunk in earthly, vain delight;
But the true-born child of God
Must not, would not, if he might.

Tune—"German Hymn."

## 56—THY WILL BE DONE.

CHARLOTTE ELLIOTT, a life-long invalid, wrote several hymns, each of which is as a chalice in which she has preserved for the consolation of other sufferers the fruit of her own prolonged affliction. Of these "Thy will be done" is the first and best.

MY God, my Father, while I stray
 Far from my home, on life's rough way,
O teach me from my heart to say,—
 Thy will be done!

If Thou shouldst call me to resign
What most I prize,—it ne'er was mine:
I only yield Thee what was Thine;
 Thy will be done!

E'en if again I ne'er should see
The friend more dear than life to me,
Ere long we both shall be with Thee;
    Thy will be done!

Should pining sickness waste away
My life in premature decay,
My Father, still I strive to say, —
    Thy will be done!

If but my fainting heart be blest
With Thy sweet Spirit for its guest,
My God, to Thee I leave the rest;
    Thy will be done!

Renew my will from day to day;
Blend it with Thine, and take away
All that now makes it hard to say
    Thy will be done!

Then, when on earth I breathe no more
The prayer oft mixed with tears before,
I'll sing upon a happier shore, —
    Thy will be done!

                TUNE — "TROYTE'S CHANT."

## 57 — MY GOD, MY FATHER, BLISSFUL NAME.

THIS famous hymn, by Miss Steele, the daughter of a Baptist minister in a Hampshire village, is described by Archdeacon Wilson, of Manchester, as the first of the three hundred which he learned as a boy, and which entered into his bone and blood as the true philosophy of life and the wisest prayer.

MY God, my Father, blissful name!
    O may I call Thee mine?
May I with sweet assurance claim
    A portion so divine?

This only can my fears control,
  And bid my sorrows fly.
What harm can ever reach my soul
  Beneath my Father's eye?

Whate'er Thy Providence denies,
  I calmly would resign,
For Thou art good and just and wise:
  O bend my will to Thine.

Whate'er Thy sacred will ordains,
  O give me strength to bear;
And let me know my Father reigns,
  And trust His tender care.

Thy sovereign ways are all unknown
  To my weak, erring sight;
Yet let my soul adoring own
  That all Thy ways are right.

My God, my Father, be Thy name
  My solace and my stay.
O wilt Thou seal my humble claim,
  And drive my fears away?

TUNE — "LINCOLN."

## 58 — O THOU, FROM WHOM ALL GOODNESS FLOWS.

THIS hymn was written by Thomas Haweis, who lived from 1732 to 1820.

O THOU, from whom all goodness flows,
  I lift my soul to Thee:
In all my sorrows, conflicts, woes,
  Good Lord, remember me.

When on my aching, burdened heart
    My sins lie heavily,
My pardon speak, new peace impart;
    In love, remember me.

When trials sore obstruct my way,
    And ills I cannot flee,
Lord, let my strength be as my day;
    For good remember me.

When worn with pain, disease, and grief,
    This feeble body see;
Grant patience, rest, and kind relief,
    Hear and remember me.

If on my face, for Thy dear name,
    Shame and reproach shall be;
All hail reproach, and welcome shame,
    If Thou remember me.

When, in the solemn hour of death,
    I wait Thy just decree,
Saviour, with my last parting breath
    I'll cry, — Remember me.

                      TUNE — "DALEHURST."

When Henry Martyn, one of the earliest and most saintly of the Protestant missionaries, was labouring in Persia, he found much consolation by repeating in his tent, amid the revilings of his persecutors: —

> If on my face, for Thy dear name
>     Shame and reproaches be,
> All hail reproach, and welcome shame,
>     If Thou remember me.

The Rev. C. H. E. White mentions, as an incident in his own experience, that "O Thou, from whom all goodness flows" was the means of the conversion of a young guardsman, who was executed for murder. His last word on the scaffold was the burden of the hymn, "Oh Lord, remember me." The rector says: "The hymn, always a favourite with me, is now very specially written on my heart, and it is a hymn which has helped me not a little."

## 59—THE EMPEROR FREDERICK'S HYMN.

When the Emperor Frederick lay dying of the cancer which made his brief reign but one long agony, he was said to have derived much help and comfort in the gloom by the following simple hymn, written by a lad of twelve, named Ernst von Willich. The boy was an invalid, and, like many others greater than he, had learnt in suffering what he taught in song. The hymn has been Englished as follows:—

IF the Lord me sorrow send,
 Let me bear it patiently;
Lifting up my heart in prayer,
Comfort He will not deny;
Therefore, let there come what will,
In the Lord my heart is still.

Though the heart is often weak,
Full of pain, and all forlorn,
Though in days of utmost pain
Not a day of joy will dawn,
Tell it, let there come what will,
In the Lord all pain is still.

So I pray, Oh Lord, my God,
Let my hope and comfort stand,
Fear nor care no more I heed,
Guided ever by Thy hand.
Therefore, let there come what will,
In the Lord my heart is still.

Tune—"Dix."

## VIII. — Salvation.

### 60 — ROCK OF AGES.

When the *Sunday at Home* took the plebiscite of 3,500 of its readers as to which were the best hymns in the language, the "Rock of Ages" stood at the top of the tree, having no fewer than 3,215 votes. Only three other hymns had more than 3,000 votes. They were, "Abide with me," "Jesu, Lover of my soul," and "Just as I am."

Rock of Ages, cleft for me,
Let me hide myself in Thee!
Let the water and the blood,
From Thy riven side which flowed,
Be of sin the double cure,
Cleanse me from its guilt and power.

Not the labours of my hands
Can fulfil Thy law's demands:
Could my zeal no respite know,
Could my tears for ever flow,
All for sin could not atone,
Thou must save, and Thou alone!

Nothing in my hand I bring;
Simply to Thy cross I cling;
Naked, come to Thee for dress;
Helpless, look to Thee for grace;
Foul, I to the fountain fly:
Wash me, Saviour, or I die!

While I draw this fleeting breath —
When my eye-strings break in death —
When I soar to worlds unknown —
See Thee on Thy judgment throne —
Rock of Ages, cleft for me,
Let me hide myself in Thee!

Tune — "Redhead, No. 76."

Toplady, a Calvinist vicar of a Devonshire parish, little dreamed that he was composing the most popular hymn in the language when he wrote what he called "A living and dying prayer for the holiest believer in the world." For Toplady was a sad polemist, whose orthodox soul was outraged by the Arminianism of the Wesleys. He and they indulged in much disputation of the brickbat and Billingsgate order, as was the fashion in those days. Toplady put much of his time and energy into the composition of controversial pamphlets, on which the good man prided himself not a little. The dust lies thick upon these his works, nor is it likely to be disturbed now or in the future. But in a pause in the fray, just by way of filling up an interval in the firing of polemical broadsides, Augustus Montague Toplady thought he saw a way of launching an airy dart at a joint in Wesley's armour, on the subject of Sanctification. So without much ado, and without any knowledge that it was by this alone he was to render permanent service to mankind, he sent off to the *Gospel Magazine* of 1776 the hymn "Rock of Ages."[1] When it appeared, he had, no doubt, considerable complacency in reflecting how he had winged his opponent for his insolent doctrine of entire sanctification, and it is probable that before he died,— for he only survived its publication by two years, dying when but thirty-eight,— he had still no conception of the relative importance of his own work. But to-day the world knows Toplady only as the writer of these four verses. All else that he laboured over it has forgotten, and indeed does well to forget.

It was this hymn which the Prince Consort asked for as he came near to death. Mr. Gladstone has trans-

[1] On the appearance of the first edition of this work a ministerial correspondent who has given considerable attention to the subject of hymnology wrote to say that this story of the hymn "Rock of Ages" was rather misleading. "Toplady," he said, "was editor of the *Gospel Magazine* at the time, and the hymn was the pendant to a curious theological article."

lated it into Latin, Greek, and Italian. Dr. Pusey declared it to be "the most deservedly popular hymn, perhaps the very favourite." The followers of Wesley, against whom the hymn was originally launched as a light missile in the polemical combat, seized it for their collection and mutilated it the while — why, does not clearly appear. The unfortunate Armenians who were butchered the other day in Constantinople sang a translation of "Rock of Ages" which, indeed, has made the tour of the world, side by side with the Bible and the Pilgrim's Progress. It is recorded that General Stuart, the dashing cavalry leader of the Southern Confederacy, sang the hymn with his dying strength, as his life slowly ebbed away from the wounds he had received in the battles before Richmond. When the "London" went down in the Bay of Biscay, Jan. 11, 1866, the last thing which the last man who left the ship heard as the boat pushed off from the doomed vessel was the voices of the passengers singing "Rock of Ages." "No other English hymn can be named which has laid so broad and firm a grasp on the English-speaking world."

## 61 — BLESSED LORD, IN THEE IS REFUGE.

IT would be impossible in any collection of hymns that have helped to ignore the hymnody of the Salvation Army. This latest birth of the religious sentiment owes at least as much of its astonishing success to its hymns as to its discipline. It has converted the ordinary 'Arry and 'Arriett first of all into Blood and Fire Soldiers, and then it has set them writing hymns. No religious denomination, no organisation of any kind has done so much to develop the verse-writing instinct latent in most men as the Salvation Army. Every week the *War Cry* is filled with new hymns, — hymns of all kinds, good, bad, and indifferent. They have long since passed the fresh and sweet simplicity of that most characteristic of all their war songs, beginning, —

> "The devil and me, We can't agree,
> I hate him, and he hates me,"—

than which nothing could possibly be more concise and graphic. Of the bards of the Army, whose name is legion, Mr. Herbert Booth is conspicuous as the author of a hymn which is worthily and deservedly popular, although it is nowhere used with such effect as in the All-night meetings, when the line "Lord, I make a full surrender," is sung over and over again until the converts empty their pockets, smash their pipes, forswear finery, and find abundant compensation for their sacrifice in the ecstasy of their religious enthusiasm, and the comradeship of the rank and file of the Salvation Army. The Volunteers of America find this hymn one of the two most helpful in their prison work, when they employ hymns at all. Usually the convicts like only refrains and choruses that cling to their memory long after the Volunteer visitors have left them. The hymn is as follows:—

> BLESSED Lord, in Thee is refuge,
>   Safety for my trembling soul,
> Power to lift my head when drooping
>   'Midst the angry billows' roll.
> I will trust Thee, All my life Thou shalt control.
>
> In the past too unbelieving
>   'Midst the tempest I have been,
> And my heart has slowly trusted
>   What my eyes have never seen.
> Blessed Jesus, Teach me on Thy arm to lean.
>
> Oh, for trust that brings the triumph
>   When defeat seems strangely near!
> Oh, for faith that changes fighting
>   Into victory's ringing cheer —
> Faith triumphant, Knowing not defeat or fear!

Welcome, welcome, dear Redeemer!
 Welcome to this heart of mine;
Lord, I make a full surrender;
 Every power and thought be Thine —
Thine entirely; Through eternal ages Thine.

Known to all to be Thy mansion,
 Earth and hell will disappear;
Or in vain attempt possession,
 When they find the Lord is there.
Shout salvation! Shout, ye saints! the Lord is here!

TUNE FROM THE SALVATION ARMY HYMN-BOOK.

A correspondent in Brentwood, who prefaced his remarks by saying, " I am not a Salvationist *à la* Booth," writes: "Hymns under all circumstances have been spiritual meat and drink to me, but the Salvation Army songs have tapped a new mine. I have felt like an old war-horse hearing the trumpet sound at mass meetings. My whole being has been stirred by the power and intensity of these wonderful compositions. The hymn that has helped me, and lifted me out of sloughs, carried me to the eternal walls, and up to heaven's gate, is 'Blessed Lord, in Thee is refuge.'"

## 62—JUST AS I AM.

THIS poem, by Charlotte Elliott, so universally known and prized, is associated indissolubly by many with the time of their conversion. Her brother, the Rev. H. V. Elliott, stated: "In the course of a long ministry I hope I have been permitted to see some fruit of my labours, but I feel far more has been done by a single hymn of my sister's." There is no language or land where the melody of this hymn is not heard. It was first published in the " Invalid's Hymn-Book " in 1836. To-day it is the most familiar formula on the lips of the

Christian evangelist in all quarters of the world. A word fitly spoken, indeed!

JUST as I am, without one plea,
But that Thy blood was shed for me,
And that Thou bidd'st me come to Thee,
  O Lamb of God, I come!

Just as I am, and waiting not
To rid my soul of one dark blot,
To Thee, whose blood can cleanse each spot,
  O Lamb of God, I come!

Just as I am, though tossed about
With many a conflict, many a doubt,
Fightings and fears within, without,
  O Lamb of God, I come!

Just as I am, poor, wretched, blind;
Sight, riches, healing of the mind,
Yea, all I need in Thee to find,
  O Lamb of God, I come!

Just as I am, Thou wilt receive,
Wilt welcome, pardon, cleanse, relieve,
Because Thy promise I believe,
  O Lamb of God, I come!

Just as I am (Thy love unknown
Has broken every barrier down),
Now to be Thine, yea, Thine alone,
  O Lamb of God, I come!

Just as I am, of that free love
The breadth, length, depth, and height to prove,
Here for a season, then above,
  O Lamb of God, I come!

TUNE — "GAINSWORTH."

## 63—HARK, MY SOUL, IT IS THE LORD.

This poem of Cowper's, Mr. Gladstone has translated into Latin.

HARK, my soul! it is the Lord;
'T is thy Saviour, hear His word;
Jesus speaks, and speaks to thee:
"Say, poor sinner, lov'st thou Me?

"I delivered thee when bound,
And, when bleeding, healed thy wound;
Sought thee wandering, set thee right,
Turned thy darkness into light.

"Can a woman's tender care
Cease towards the child she bare?
Yes, she may forgetful be,
Yet will I remember thee.

"Mine is an unchanging love,
Higher than the heights above;
Deeper than the depths beneath,
Free and faithful, strong as death.

"Thou shalt see My glory soon,
When the work of grace is done;
Partner of My throne shalt be:
Say, poor sinner, lov'st thou Me?"

Lord, it is my chief complaint
That my love is cold and faint,
Yet I love Thee and adore,
O for grace to love Thee more!

TUNE—"ST. BEES."

Archdeacon Sinclair mentions this as one of the two hymns which he has found most useful, the second being Bishop Ken's "Evening Hymn." Archdeacon

Sinclair says: "'Hark, my Soul' is the most beautiful of all English hymns. It emphasises what is the essence of the Christian faith, — the appeal of Christ to the individual man. It describes in language that is exquisitely simple and true the work of the Saviour for the soul in redemption. In words hardly less powerful than those of St. Paul, it brings home to the heart the truth that He who speaks to us through the Gospel is the fulness of Him who filleth all in all, and then it closes by bringing the poor human heart, conscious of its own feebleness, into its true attitude of absolute reliance on the Divine peace, in which it lives and moves, and has its being."

## 64—O LOVE, THAT WILT NOT LET ME GO.

A CORRESPONDENT, writing from Scotland, pleads for Dr. Matheson's hymn, which begins with "O Love, that wilt not let me go," and says: "At a time of great spiritual darkness, when God, Christ, and Heaven seemed to have gone out of my life, and neither sun nor stars in many days appeared, after months of hopeless misery of mind, I heard this hymn sung in a little country chapel. The first two lines haunted me for weeks, and at last brought light and comfort to my dark soul."

A Presbyterian minister says: "More than any other hymn it appeals to me," for a reason altogether different from that of the previous correspondent. "Amongst students of philosophy Hegel is always gaining appreciation. This hymn is Hegelianism in verse."

O LOVE, that wilt not let me go,
    I rest my weary soul on Thee;
I give Thee back the life I owe,
That in Thine ocean depth its flow
    May richer, fuller be.

O Light, that followest all my way,
    I yield my flickering torch to Thee;

My heart restores its borrowed ray,
That in Thy sunshine's blaze its day
    May brighter, fairer be.

O Joy, that seekest me through pain,
  I cannot close my heart to Thee;
I trace the rainbow through the rain,
And feel the promise is not vain,
    That morn shall fearless be.

O Cross, that liftest up my head,
  I dare not ask to fly from Thee;
I lay in dust life's glory dead,
And from the ground there blossoms red
    Life that shall endless be.

          TUNE—"ST. MARGARET."

## 65—WHEN I SURVEY THE WONDROUS CROSS.

THIS is one of the four hymns which stand at the head of all hymns in the English language. Here is the hymn as Dr. Watts wrote it:—

WHEN I survey the wondrous Cross,
  On which the Prince of glory died,
My richest gain I count but loss,
And pour contempt on all my pride.

Forbid it, Lord, that I should boast,
Save in the Cross of Christ my God;
All the vain things that charm me most,
I sacrifice them to His blood.

See from His Head, His Hands, His Feet,
Sorrow and love flow mingled down;
Did e'er such love and sorrow meet,
Or thorns compose so rich a crown?

His dying crimson, like a robe,
Spreads o'er His body on the tree;
Then am I dead to all the world,
And all the world is dead to me!

Were the whole realm of nature mine,
That were a present far too small;
Love so amazing, so Divine,
Demands my soul, my life, my all.

TUNE — "ROCKINGHAM."

This is said to be Watts's finest hymn. Julian puts it as one of the four which, for popular use, stand at the head of all other English hymns, the other three being Ken's "Morning Hymn," "Hark, the Herald Angels," and "Rock of Ages." Mrs. Evans, the original of George Eliot's Dinah in "Adam Bede," quoted the third verse when dying. Father Ignatius, when preaching at the Church of St. Edmund the King, Lombard Street, slowly repeated the last line after the congregation had sung it, and added, "Well, I am surprised to hear you sing that. Do you know that altogether you only put fifteen shillings into the bag this morning?"

## 66 — THERE IS A FOUNTAIN FILLED WITH BLOOD.

THERE is a fountain filled with blood,
    Drawn from Immanuel's veins;
And sinners plunged beneath that flood
    Lose all their guilty stains.

The dying thief rejoiced to see
    That fountain in his day;
And there may I, though vile as he,
    Wash all my sins away.

Dear dying Lamb, Thy precious blood
    Shall never lose its power,

Till the whole ransomed church of God
  Be saved, to sin no more.

E'er since, by faith, I saw the stream
  Thy flowing wounds supply,
Redeeming love has been my theme,
  And shall be till I die.

Then in a nobler, sweeter song,
  I'll sing Thy power to save;
When this poor lisping, stammering tongue
  Lies silent in the grave.

            TUNE — "WILTSHIRE" OR "HORSLEY."

"This hymn," writes a correspondent, "was one which first opened my eyes to the need of a Saviour, and brought me also to the Christ. I have seen a thousand hard hearts broken down by the singing of the hymn and the realising of that picture."

Rev. James Spurgeon writes: "This hymn has spoken to my heart as no other hymn has done. The revival chorus,

> I do believe, I will believe,
>   That Jesus died for me,
> And by His blood, His precious blood,
>   From sin has set me free,

should be added to this hymn."

Cowper's famous hymn has been fiercely assailed. "This hymn," says Sir Edwin Arnold, editor of the *Daily Telegraph* and author of "The Light of Asia," is absolutely shocking to my mind." Thousands of sensitive minds in the United States reject words so revolting. Mr. Bird, of Glasgow, denounced it fiercely as "the language of the shambles."

But, as Mr. Price Hughes wrote me sententiously, "if it has been much criticised it has been much blessed." All the animadversions of Matthew Arnold, for instance, are as the lightest dust of the balance compared with the fact of the marvellous influence which the singing of this hymn has had in softening the heart of man upon such occasions of spiritual quickening as are known as the great Irish Revivals. It has been the means of changing the lives of more men than all those who have ever heard the name of most of its critics, and it is not surprising that it has forced its way by sheer influence of spiritual power into such hymnals as "Ancient and Modern" and the Methodist collection, from which it had been jealously excluded, in the one case till 1889, and in the other till 1876.

## 67—GRACIOUS SPIRIT, HOLY GHOST.

This paraphrase of 1 Cor. xiii., by Bishop Wordsworth of Lincoln was first published in 1862. Unitarians sing a version beginning " Mighty Spirit, Gracious Guide."

GRACIOUS Spirit, Holy Ghost,
   Taught by Thee, we covet most
Of Thy gifts at Pentecost,
   Holy, heavenly love.

Faith that mountains could remove,
Tongues of earth or heaven above,
Knowledge — all things — empty prove
   Without Heavenly Love.

Though I as a martyr bleed,
Give my goods the poor to feed,
All is vain, if love I need;
   Therefore give me love.

Love is kind, and suffers long,
Love is meek, and thinks no wrong,
Love than death itself more strong;
   Therefore give us love.

Prophecy will fade away,
Melting in the light of day;
Love will ever with us stay;
  Therefore give us love.

Faith will vanish into sight;
Hope be emptied in delight;
Love in Heav'n will shine more bright:
  Therefore give us love.

Faith and hope and love we see
Joining hand in hand agree.
But the greatest of the three,
  And the best is love.

From the overshadowing
Of Thy gold and silver wing,
Shed on us, who to Thee sing,
  Holy, heavenly love.   Amen.

TUNE — "CHARITY."

## 68—JESU, LOVER OF MY SOUL.

THIS is Charles Wesley's masterpiece. "I would rather have written this hymn," says Henry Ward Beecher, "than to have the fame of all the kings that ever sat on the earth. . . . That hymn will go on singing until the last trump brings forth the angel-band; and then, I think, it will mount up on some lip to the very presence of God."

JESU! Lover of my soul,
    Let me to Thy bosom fly,
While the nearer waters roll,
    While the tempest still is high;
Hide me, O my Saviour, hide,
    Till the storm of life is past;
Safe into the haven guide:
    O receive my soul at last!

Other refuge have I none;
  Hangs my helpless soul on Thee;
Leave, ah! leave me not alone,
  Still support and comfort me.
All my trust on Thee is stayed;
  All my help from Thee I bring;
Cover my defenceless head
  With the shadow of Thy wing.

Wilt Thou not regard my call?
  Wilt Thou not accept my prayer?
Lo! I sink, I faint, I fall,
  Lo! on Thee I cast my care,
Reach me out Thy gracious hand!
  While I of Thy strength receive,
Hoping against hope I stand,
  Dying, and behold I live!

Thou, O Christ, art all I want;
  More than all in Thee I find;
Raise the fallen, cheer the faint,
  Heal the sick and lead the blind.
Just and Holy is Thy name;
  I am all unrighteousness:
False and full of sin I am;
  Thou art full of truth and grace.

Plenteous grace with Thee is found,
  Grace to cover all my sin;
Let the healing streams abound,
  Make and keep me pure within.
Thou of life the fountain art,
  Freely let me take of Thee;
Spring Thou up within my heart,
  Rise, to all eternity.

                    TUNE — "HOLLINGSIDE."

Round this hymn are gathering the delightful traditions which convert the driest facts into fascinating fairy tales. There is no end to the stories which good Methodists will tell you as to how this hymn has helped poor mortals in the hour and article of death. Shipwrecked captains read it before they perish in the deep. A mother and child lashed upon a spar float down the Channel, the poor woman lifts her feeble voice singing this hymn, and she is rescued. Passengers on board a steamer in the heart of a thunderstorm allay panic and prepare for death amid blinding sheets of flame and bursts of thunder by raising the familiar tune. Dr. Lyman Beecher dies listening to the first two lines as they were read to him by his wife. It is, they say, the finest heart hymn in the English language. As befits a poem so freely incrusted with traditions, it has a suitable legendary origin. It is said that "Charles Wesley was sitting at his desk when a bird pursued by a hawk flew into the open window. The baffled hawk did not dare to follow, and the poet took his pen and wrote this immortal song."

## 69 — OUR BLEST REDEEMER, ERE HE BREATHED.

THIS hymn by Harriet Auber dates from 1829. It is very popular, and has been translated into many languages.

OUR Blest Redeemer, ere He breathed
    His tender last farewell,
A Guide, a Comforter, bequeath'd
    With us to dwell.

He came in semblance of a dove,
    With sheltering wings outspread,
The holy balm of peace and love
    On each to shed.

He came in tongues of living fire
    To teach, convince, subdue;
All powerful as the wind He came —
    As viewless too.

He came sweet influence to impart,
    A gracious, willing Guest,
While He can find one humble heart
    Wherein to rest.

And His that gentle voice we hear,
    Soft as the breath of even,
That checks each fault, that calms each fear,
    And speaks of Heaven.

And every virtue we possess,
    And every conquest won,
And every thought of holiness,
    Are His alone.

Spirit of purity and grace,
    Our weakness pitying see;
O make our hearts Thy dwelling place,
    And meet for Thee.

              TUNE — "ST. CUTHBERT."

## 70 — COME, O THOU TRAVELLER UNKNOWN.

COME, O Thou Traveller unknown,
    Whom still I hold but cannot see;
My company before is gone,
    And I am left alone with Thee;
With Thee all night I mean to stay,
And wrestle till the break of day.

I need not tell Thee who I am,
    My misery or sin declare;

Thyself hast called me by my name;
  Look on Thy hands and read it there;
But who, I ask Thee, who art Thou?
Tell me Thy name, and tell me now.

In vain Thou strugglest to get free,
  I never will unloose my hold:
Art Thou the Man that died for me?
  The secret of Thy love unfold:
Wrestling, I will not let Thee go,
Till I Thy name, Thy nature know.

What though my shrinking flesh complain,
  And murmur to contend so long,
I rise superior to my pain;
  When I am weak then I am strong;
And when my all of strength shall fail,
I shall with the God-man prevail.

Yield to me now, for I am weak,
  But confident in self-despair;
Speak to my heart, in blessings speak;
  Be conquered by my instant prayer!
Speak, or Thou never hence shalt move,
And tell me, if Thy name is Love?

'Tis Love! 'tis Love! Thou diedst for me!
  I hear Thy whisper in my heart;
The morning breaks, the shadows flee;
  Pure, universal Love Thou art;
To me, to all, Thy mercies move;
Thy nature and Thy name is Love.

TUNE — "PENIEL."

"Of equal poetic value to Xavier's hymn," wrote Mr. Massingham, the editor of the *Daily Chronicle*, "is Charles Wesley's extraordinary poem, which, though it is sung as a hymn, is rather a mystical rhapsody, full of colour and imagination, beginning —

  'Come, O thou traveller unknown,
   Whom still I hold but cannot see.'"

Mr. Moncure D. Conway says: "I can remember in my old Methodist days how much (as doubts grew) I was helped by Charles Wesley's hymn, 'Come, O Thou Traveller Unknown.'"

Mr. Price Hughes declares it is one of Wesley's greatest hymns, and recalls the fact that it was quoted with great effect by Dean Stanley when he unveiled Wesley's memorial in Westminster Abbey. Dr. Watts said that this hymn was "worth all the verses he himself had ever written."

## IX. — Consecration.

### 71 — XAVIER'S HYMN.

ONE of the best hymns in the world is that written by the Jesuit missionary, Francis Xavier, who died, worn out by his heroic labours, near Canton, in 1522. It is found in most Protestant hymn-books, and is part of the spiritual treasure of many a good soul blissfully unaware that its author was a Jesuit, and a very prince among the Brotherhood. But that is one of the blessed characteristics of hymns. The service of praise, as Beecher long ago remarked, is the one branch of Christianity where schisms have not disturbed the unity of the Catholic Church. I print Xavier's hymn in the original Latin, and in Caswall's English translation.

  MY God, I love Thee; not because
   I hope for heaven thereby,
  Nor yet because who love Thee not
   Are lost eternally.

Thou, O my Jesus, Thou didst me
  Upon the cross embrace;
For me didst bear the nails and spear,
  And manifold disgrace;

And griefs and torments numberless,
  And sweat of agony, —
Yea, death itself; and all for me,
  Who was Thine enemy.

Then why, O blessed Jesus Christ,
  Should I not love Thee well?
Not for the sake of winning heaven,
  Nor of escaping hell.

Not from the hope of gaining aught,
  Not seeking a reward;
But as Thyself hast loved me,
  O ever-loving Lord!

So would I love Thee, dearest Lord,
  And in Thy praise will sing;
Solely because Thou art my God,
  And my most loving King.

O DEUS, ego amo Te;
  Nec amo Te ut salves me,
Aut quia non amantes Te
  Aeterno punis igne.

Tu, Tu, mi Iesu, totum me
  Amplexus es in cruce;
Tulisti clavos, lanceam,
Multamque ignominiam,
  Innumeros dolores,
  Sudores et angores,
Ac mortem, et haec propter me,
  Ac pro me, peccatore.

> Cur igitur non amem Te,
> O Iesu amantissime?
> Non ut in coelo salves me,
> Aut ne aeternum damnes me,
> Nec praemii ullius spe,
> Sed sicut Tu amâsti me,
> Sic amo et amabo Te,
> Solum quia Rex meus es,
> Et solum quia Deus es.
>
> TUNE—"ST. FRANCIS XAVIER."

## 72—NEARER, MY GOD, TO THEE.

THIS is the favourite hymn of the Prince of Wales. When I wrote round to many well-known people asking them which hymn helped them most, I received the following reply from the Prince:—

> SANDRINGHAM, NORFOLK,
> December 29th, 1895.
>
> DEAR MR. STEAD,—The Prince of Wales desires me to thank you for your letter, and to say that he fully appreciates the compliment you pay him when you ask him to assist you in your proposed work. His Royal Highness would have gladly lent his aid if it had been in his power, but he fears that an opportunity for doing so will hardly be given him. He directs me to mention that among serious hymns he thinks there is none more touching nor one that goes more truly to the heart than No. 7 on your list: "Nearer, my God, to Thee."—Believe me, yours very truly,
>
> FRANCIS KNOLLYS.

The selection is interesting on many grounds. "Nearer, my God, to Thee" was written by a woman, that woman a Unitarian, and that Unitarian the daughter of a couple who first met in Newgate Gaol, where her father had been sent to lie for six months as atonement for the heinous crime of defending the French

# HYMNS THAT HAVE HELPED. 159

Revolution and criticising the political conduct of a certain Bishop Watson, now fortunately forgotten. Perhaps the sole permanent result and chief end of this Bishop Watson's life was to contribute remotely and unintentionally to the production of this hymn. He was a not unimportant link in the chain of circumstances of which this hymn, with its far-reaching influence, is but the latest outcome. For instance, if Mr. Flower — Mrs. Adams's maiden name was Flower — had not been moved to indignation by the turpitude of Bishop Watson's political conduct, he would never, even in 1789, have been fined £100 and sent to Newgate for six months. If he had never been sent to gaol, Miss Eliza Gould would never have been prompted to visit him there, and so lay the foundation of an acquaintance which ripened into love and marriage. Of that marriage Mrs. Adams was the fruit. If her parents had never met, of course she would never have been born, and this hymn never would have been written. Therefore may we not say that the *causa causans* of one of the most touching hymns in the Christian hymnal was some long-ago-forgotten political offence perpetrated by an Anglican Bishop. Here is the hymn as Mrs. Adams wrote it, untinkered by jealous Trinitarians who feel twinges of conscience at the thought of deriving spiritual benefit from a Unitarian hymn.

NEARER, my God, to Thee,
   Nearer to Thee!
E'en though it be a cross
   That raiseth me,
Still all my song shall be,
Nearer, my God, to Thee, —
   Nearer to Thee!

Though, like the wanderer,
   Daylight all gone,
Darkness be over me,
   My rest a stone:

Yet in my dreams I'd be
Nearer, my God, to Thee,—
   Nearer to Thee!

There let the way appear
   Steps unto heaven;
All that Thou send'st to me,
   In mercy given;
Angels to beckon me
Nearer, my God, to Thee,—
   Nearer to Thee!

Then with my waking thoughts
   Bright with Thy praise,
Out of my stony griefs
   Bethel I'll raise:
So by my woes to be
Nearer, my God, to Thee,—
   Nearer to Thee!

Or if on joyful wing,
   Cleaving the sky,
Sun, moon, and stars forgot,
   Upward I fly;
Still, still, my song shall be,
Nearer, my God, to Thee,—
   Nearer to Thee!

                    TUNE—"HORBURY."

    The hymn is as dear to the peasant as it is to the prince. Bishop Marvin, wandering homeless in Arkansas during the war, and almost inclined to despair, found himself marvellously cheered and reproved when in the midst of the wilderness he overheard a widowed old woman singing, "Nearer, my God, to Thee" in the midst of a dilapidated log cabin. Her wretched poverty was forgotten as she sang.

Another story of the American Civil War tells how a little drummer boy, whose arm had been shot off at the battle of Fort Donelson, died on the battlefield singing with his last breath, "Nearer, my God, to Thee." It might fairly be called the most popular hymn among all sorts and conditions of men in America.

## 73—TAKE MY LIFE, AND LET IT BE.

AFTER the Jesuit and the Unitarian comes the devout Churchwoman. Miss Havergal's hymn is not unworthy of its predecessors.

TAKE my life, and let it be
Consecrated, Lord, to Thee.
Take my moments and my days,
Let them flow in ceaseless praise.

Take my hands and let them move
At the impulse of Thy love.
Take my feet and let them be
Swift and beautiful for Thee.

Take my voice, and let me sing
Always, only, for my King.
Take my lips, and let them be,
Filled with messages from Thee.

Take my silver and my gold,
Not a mite would I withhold.
Take my intellect and use
Every power as Thou dost choose.

Take my will and make it Thine;
It shall be no longer mine.
Take my heart, it is Thine own;
It shall be Thy royal throne.

Take my love: my Lord, I pour
At Thy feet its treasure-store.
Take myself, and I will be
Ever, only, all for Thee!

TUNE—"ST. BEES."

This hymn bubbled up from the depths of a thankful heart. Miss Havergal tells the story of how it came to be written:—

"Perhaps you will be interested to know the origin of the consecration hymn, 'Take my life.' I went for a little visit of five days. There were ten persons in the house, some unconverted and long prayed for, some converted, but not rejoicing Christians. He gave me the prayer, 'Lord, give me *all* in this house!' And He just *did*. Before I left the house every one had got a blessing. The last night of my visit I was too happy to sleep, and passed most of the night in praise and renewal of my own consecration, and these little couplets formed themselves and chimed in my heart, one after another, till they finished with 'Ever, only, all for Thee.'"

## 74—O FOR A HEART TO PRAISE MY GOD.

CHARLES WESLEY'S hymn is in unison with those which precede it.

O FOR a heart to praise my God;
  A heart from sin set free;
A heart that's sprinkled with the blood
  So freely shed for me.

A heart resigned, submissive, meek,
  My dear Redeemer's throne:
Where only Christ is heard to speak:
  Where Jesus reigns alone.

A humble, lowly, contrite heart,
  Believing, true, and clean,

Which neither life nor death can part
  From Him that dwells within.

A heart in every thought renewed,
  And filled with love divine;
Perfect and right, and pure and good;
  A copy, Lord, of Thine.

Thy nature, gracious Lord, impart,
  Come quickly from above:
Write Thy new name upon my heart,—
  Thy new best name of Love.

TUNE—"WINCHESTER OLD."

## 75—O GOD OF TRUTH.

THIS is Tom Hughes's hymn, which, says Mr. Horder, "seems to gather up and embody the distinctive thoughts and feelings which animated his life. It was probably suggested by Maurice's sermon, 'the Word of God conquering through Sacrifice.'"

O GOD of Truth, Whose living word
    Upholds whate'er hath breath,
  Look down on Thy creation, Lord,
    Enslaved by sin and death.

Set up Thy standard, Lord, that they
  Who claim a heavenly birth
May march with Thee to smite the lies
  That vex Thy ransom'd earth.

Ah! would we join that blest array,
  And follow in the might
Of Him, the Faithful and the True,
  In raiment clean and white?

*We* fight for truth, *we* fight for God,
  Poor slaves of lies and sin,

He who would fight for Thee on Earth,
  Must first be true within.

Then, God of Truth, for Whom we long —
  Thou Who wilt hear our prayer —
Do Thine own battle in our hearts,
  And slay the falsehood there.

Still smite! still burn! till naught is left
  But God's own truth and love;
Then, Lord, as morning dew come down,
  Rest on us from above.

Yea, come! then, tried as in the fire,
  From every lie set free,
Thy perfect truth shall dwell in us,
  And we shall live in Thee.        Amen.

TUNE — "TALLIS."

## 76—O FOR A CLOSER WALK WITH GOD.

"THIS is one of the most beautiful, tender, and popular of all Cowper's hymns." — Julian's "Dictionary of Hymnology."

O FOR a closer walk with God!
  A calm and heavenly frame;
A light to shine upon the road
  That leads me to the Lamb!

Where is the blessedness I knew
  When first I saw the Lord?
Where is the soul-refreshing view
  Of Jesus and His word?

What peaceful hours I once enjoyed!
  How sweet their memory still!
But they have left an aching void
  The world can never fill.

Return, O holy Dove, return!
  Sweet messenger of rest;
I hate the sins that made Thee mourn,
  And drove Thee from my breast:

The dearest idol I have known,
  Whate'er that idol be,
Help me to tear it from Thy throne,
  And worship only Thee.

So shall my walk be close with God,
  Calm and serene my frame:
So purer light shall mark the road
  That leads me to the Lamb.

TUNE—"MARTYRDOM."

## 77—O JESUS, I HAVE PROMISED.

THIS is a popular Confirmation hymn, which was contributed by the late Rev. J. E. Bode in 1869 to the "Psalms and Hymns," published by the Society for Promoting Christian Knowledge.

O JESUS, I have promised
  To serve Thee to the end;
Be Thou for ever near me,
  My Master and my Friend;
I shall not fear the battle
  If Thou art by my side,
Nor wander from the pathway
  If Thou wilt be my Guide.

O let me feel Thee near me:
  The world is ever near;
I see the sights that dazzle,
  The tempting sounds I hear.
My foes are ever near me,
  Around me and within;

But, Jesus, draw Thou nearer,
  And shield my soul from sin.

O let me hear Thee speaking
  In accents clear and still,
Above the storms of passion,
  The murmurs of self-will:
O speak to re-assure me,
  To hasten or control;
O speak, and make me listen,
  Thou Guardian of my soul.

O Jesus, Thou hast promised
  To all who follow Thee,
That where Thou art in glory
  There shall Thy servant be;
And, Jesus, I have promised
  To serve Thee to the end
O give me grace to follow,
  My Master and my Friend.

O let me see Thy foot-marks,
  And in them plant mine own;
My hope to follow duly
  Is in Thy strength alone;
O guide me, call me, draw me,
  Uphold me to the end;
And then in Heav'n receive me,
  My Saviour and my Friend.  Amen.

TUNE—"DAY OF REST."

## 78—OH TO BE NOTHING, NOTHING.

THIS is one of the most popular of modern hymns.

A lady who worked among the girls in business houses in the West of England for twelve years, said: "It is always surprising to hear and discover what were the hymns which seemed to help the girls and which did not. One of them which seemed to be most helpful was this, 'Oh to be nothing, nothing.'" The authoress herself writes: "It has always been a wonder to me why that helped people under such varied circumstances. Prof. Rendell Harris has often told me how much he has owed to that hymn. I could show you, were it not breaking confidences, a sheaf of letters giving testimony to the help which that hymn has been to all sorts and conditions of men and women — Roman Catholics, Unitarians, High Churchmen, Dissenters — under all kinds of circumstances." It has been translated into many languages, and has circulated far and wide, meeting everywhere with immense acceptance.

OH to be nothing, nothing!
  Only to lie at His feet,
A broken and emptied vessel,
  For the Master's use made meet.
Emptied — that He might fill me,
  As forth to His service I go;
Broken — that so unhindered
  His life through me might flow.

Oh to be nothing, nothing!
  Only as led by His hand;
A messenger at His gateway,
  Only waiting for His command:
Only an instrument ready
  His praises to sound at His will;
Willing, should He not require me,
  In silence to wait on Him still.

Oh to be nothing, nothing!
  Painful the humbling may be,
Yet low in the dust I'd lay me
  That the world might my Saviour see.

## 168 HYMNS THAT HAVE HELPED.

> Rather be nothing, nothing!
>   To Him let our voices be raised:
>   He is the Fountain of blessing,
>   He only is meet to be praised.
>
>     TUNE FROM "SONGS AND SOLOS."

# X. — The Warfare of Life.

### 79—ONWARD, CHRISTIAN SOLDIERS.

THE Duke of Cambridge, late Commander-in-Chief of the British Army, mentioned this processional hymn by the Rev. S. Baring-Gould as his favourite.

ONWARD, Christian soldiers! marching as to war,
With the Cross of Jesus, going on before.
Christ, the Royal Master, leads against the foe;
Forward into battle see His banners go.
  Onward, Christian soldiers! marching as to war,
  With the Cross of Jesus, going on before.

At the sign of triumph, Satan's host doth flee;
On then, Christian soldiers, on to victory!
Hell's foundations quiver at the shout of praise:
Brothers, lift your voices, loud your anthems raise!

Like a mighty army moves the church of God:
Brothers, we are treading where the saints have trod;
We are not divided, all one body we—
One in hope and doctrine, one in charity.

Crowns and thrones may perish, kingdoms rise and wane;
But the church of Jesus constant will remain;

Gates of hell can never 'gainst that church prevail;
We have Christ's own promise — and that cannot
  fail.

Onward then, ye people, join our happy throng;
Blend with ours your voices in the triumph-song:
" Glory, laud, and honour, unto Christ the King "—
This through countless ages men and angels sing.
TUNE — "ST. GERTRUDE."

## 80 — OFT IN SORROW, OFT IN WOE.

KIRKE WHITE'S marching song of the Christian Life has no such lilting tune attached to it as "Onward, Christian Soldiers," but being older it has probably helped more souls than its recent rival.

OFT in sorrow, oft in woe,
  Onward, Christians, onward go;
Fight the fight, maintain the strife,
Strengthened with the bread of life.

Let your drooping hearts be glad;
March in heavenly armour clad;
Fight, nor think the battle long,
Soon shall victory tune your song.

Let not sorrow dim your eye,
Soon shall every tear be dry;
Let not fears your course impede,
Great your strength if great your need.

Onward, then, to glory move,
More than conquerors ye shall prove;
Though opposed by many a foe,
Christian soldiers, onward go.
TUNE — "EPHRAIM."

## 81—SOLDIERS OF CHRIST, ARISE!

This hymn by Charles Wesley is inspiriting as the blast of the bugle:—

SOLDIERS of Christ, arise!
   And put your armour on,
Strong in the strength which God supplies
   Through His eternal Son.

Strong in the Lord of Hosts,
   And in His mighty power;
Who in the strength of Jesus trusts
   Is more than conqueror.

Stand then in His great might,
   With all His strength endued;
And take, to arm you for the fight,
   The panoply of God.

From strength to strength go on;
   Wrestle, and fight, and pray;
Tread all the powers of darkness down,
   And win the well-fought day;

That having all things done,
   And all your conflicts past,
Ye may o'ercome through Christ alone,
   And stand complete at last.

                            TUNE—"GILDAS."

## 82—CHRISTIAN! SEEK NOT YET REPOSE.

Another of Charlotte Elliott's hymns which has achieved no little popularity.

"CHRISTIAN! seek not yet repose,"
   Hear thy guardian Angel say:
Thou art in the midst of foes;
   "Watch and pray."

Principalities and powers,
Mustering their unseen array,
Wait for thy unguarded hours:
   "Watch and pray."

Gird thy heavenly armour on,
Wear it ever night and day;
Ambush'd lies the evil one;
   "Watch and pray."

Hear the victors who o'ercame;
Still they mark each warrior's way:
All with one sweet voice exclaim,
   "Watch and pray."

Hear, above all, hear thy Lord,
Him thou lovest to obey;
Hide within thy heart His Word,
   "Watch and pray."

Watch, as if on that alone
Hung the issue of the day;
Pray that help may be sent down;
   "Watch and pray."   Amen.

                TUNE—"VIGILANTE."

## 83—FORWARD! BE OUR WATCHWORD.

DEAN ALFORD's processional hymn is a universal favourite.

FORWARD! be our watchword,
   Steps and voices joined;
Seek the things before us,
   Not a look behind;
Burns the fiery pillar
   At our army's head;

# HYMNS THAT HAVE HELPED.

Who shall dream of shrinking,
  By our Captain led?
Forward through the desert,
  Through the toil and fight;
Jordan flows before us,
  Zion beams with light.

Forward, flock of Jesus,
  Salt of all the earth,
Till each yearning purpose
  Spring to glorious birth:
Sick, they ask for healing;
  Blind, they grope for day:
Pour upon the nations
  Wisdom's loving ray.
Forward, out of error;
  Leave behind the night;
Forward through the darkness,
  Forward into light.

Glories upon glories
  Hath our God prepared,
By the souls that love Him
  One day to be shared:
Eye hath not beheld them,
  Ear hath never heard;
Nor of these hath uttered
  Thought or speech a word:
Forward, marching eastward,
  Where the heaven is bright,
Till the veil be lifted,
  Till our faith be sight.

Far o'er yon horizon
  Rise the city towers,
Where our God abideth;
  That fair home is ours.

Flash the streets with jasper,
  Shine the gates with gold;
Flows the gladdening river,
  Shedding joys untold;
Thither, onward thither,
  In the Spirit's might:
Pilgrims to your country,
  Forward into light.

To the Eternal Father
  Loudest anthems raise;
To the Son and Spirit
  Echo songs of praise;
To the Lord of Glory,
  Blessèd Three in One,
Be by men and angels
  Endless honours done.
Weak are earthly praises,
  Dull the songs of night;
Forward into triumph,
  Forward into light.

TUNE—"ST. BONIFACE" OR "ST. GERTRUDE."

## XI.—Missions, Home and Foreign.

### 84—FROM GREENLAND'S ICY MOUNTAINS.

THIS hymn was written by Heber at short notice in 1819. Dean Shipley asked him one Saturday to prepare some verses to be sung at the missionary service to be held next morning. Heber sat down and dashed off these verses, which speedily became the favourite missionary hymn of the English-speaking world.

FROM Greenland's icy mountains,
  From India's coral strand,
Where Afric's sunny fountains
  Roll down their golden sand,

From many an ancient river,
    From many a palmy plain,
They call us to deliver
    Their land from error's chain.

What though the spicy breezes
    Blow soft o'er Ceylon's isle;
Though every prospect pleases,
    And only man is vile;
In vain, with lavish kindness,
    The gifts of God are strown;
The heathen, in his blindness,
    Bows down to wood and stone.

Can we, whose souls are lighted
    With wisdom from on high, —
Can we to men benighted
    The lamp of life deny?
Salvation! O salvation!
    The joyful sound proclaim,
Till each remotest nation
    Has learned Messiah's name.

Waft, waft, ye winds, His story;
    And you, ye waters, roll,
Till, like a sea of glory,
    It spreads from pole to pole;
Till, o'er our ransomed nature,
    The Lamb for sinners slain,
Redeemer, King, Creator,
    In bliss return to reign.

                    TUNE — "MISSIONARY."

## 85 — JESUS SHALL REIGN WHERE'ER THE SUN.

AFTER "From Greenland's icy mountains," this paraphrase by Watts of part of Psalm lxxii. has helped the missionary cause most. It is at once a psalm and a prophecy.

> JESUS shall reign where'er the sun
> Doth his successive journeys run :
> His kingdom stretch from shore to shore,
> Till moons shall wax and wane no more.
>
> For Him shall endless prayer be made,
> And praises throng to crown His head;
> His name like sweet perfume shall rise
> With every morning sacrifice.
>
> People and realms of every tongue
> Dwell on His love with sweetest song ;
> And infant voices shall proclaim
> Their early blessings on His name.
>
> Blessings abound where'er He reigns :
> The prisoner leaps to loose his chains ;
> The weary find eternal rest,
> And all the sons of want are blest.
>
> Where He displays His healing power,
> Death and the curse are known no more ;
> In Him the tribes of Adam boast
> More blessings than their father lost.
>
> TUNE—"THE OLD HUNDREDTH."

When, in 1862, King George, one of the converts of the English missionaries in the South Sea Islands, substituted a Christian for a Pagan constitution for his country, 5,000 natives who were gathered at the ceremonial joined as with one voice in singing this hymn.

## 86—THERE WERE NINETY AND NINE.

THIS hymn, although first popularised by Mr. Sankey, was written by Elizabeth C. Clephane at Melrose, in 1868. Six years afterwards, her poem, originally contributed to the *Children's Hour*, was copied into the *Christian Age*. There it was seen by Mr. Sankey, and one day, at the close of an unusually impressive meeting in Edinburgh, Mr. Sankey put the hymn verses before him, touched the keys of the organ, and sang, not knowing where he was going to come out. He finished the first verse amid profound silence. He took a long breath and wondered if he could sing the second the same way. He tried it and succeeded. After that it was easy to sing it. When he finished the hymn the meeting was all "broken down." Mr. Sankey says it was the most intense moment of his life.

THERE were ninety and nine that safely lay
    In the shelter of the fold;
But one was out on the hills away,
    Far off from the gates of gold.
Away on the mountains wild and bare,
Away from the tender Shepherd's care.

" Lord, Thou hast here Thy ninety and nine,
    Are they not enough for Thee?"
But the Shepherd made answer, " This of Mine
    Has wandered away from Me;
And although the road be rough and steep,
I go to the desert to find My sheep."

But none of the ransomed ever knew
    How deep were the waters crossed;
Nor how dark was the night that the Lord passed
    through,
    Ere he found His sheep that was lost.
Out in the desert He heard its cry,
Sick, and helpless, and ready to die.

" Lord, whence are those blood-drops all the way,
    That mark out the mountain's track?"
" They were shed for one who had gone astray
    Ere the Shepherd could bring him back."

" Lord, whence are Thy hands so rent and torn ? "
" They are pierced to-night by many a thorn."
But all through the mountains, thunder-riven,
   And up from the rocky steep,
There arose a cry to the gate of heaven,
   " Rejoice ! I have found my sheep."
And the angels echoed around the Throne,
" Rejoice ! for the Lord brings back His own."
TUNE BY IRA D. SANKEY.

## 87—ALMOST PERSUADED.

THE sad, wistful wail of the music to which this hymn was set has made it an instrument of power to many souls. The task of clinching a decision almost crystallised into action is one of the most necessary and difficult of all the tasks of the religious teacher. In its performance, such hymns as this have proved too useful to permit their exclusion on the pedantic ground that they are not addressed to the Deity. The purists are in danger of provoking a reaction which will result in objections being taken to any hymns which are not directly addressed to those whose course may be altered by touching melody or sacred song.

"ALMOST persuaded : " now to believe ;
   " Almost persuaded " Christ to receive :
  Seems now some soul to say ? —
  " Go, Spirit, go Thy way :
  Some more convenient day
    On Thee I 'll call."

" Almost persuaded : " come, come to-day !
" Almost persuaded : " turn not away !
  Jesus invites you here,
  Angels are lingering near,
  Prayers rise from hearts so dear,
    O wanderer, come !

"Almost persuaded:" harvest is past!
"Almost persuaded:" doom comes at last!
"Almost" cannot avail;
"Almost" is but to fail;
Sad, sad, that bitter wail —
"Almost" — *but lost!*

TUNE BY MR. BLISS.

## 88 — TIME IS EARNEST.

THIS is one of the anonymous hymns of the world. It belongs to the hortative class, appealing to those who sing it and who hear it sung. It first appeared in 1851, and has done much good.

TIME is earnest, passing by;
  Death is earnest, drawing nigh:
Sinner, wilt thou trifling be?
Time and death appeal to thee.

Life is earnest; when 't is o'er,
Thou returnest never more.
Soon to meet eternity,
Wilt thou never serious be?

God is earnest: kneel and pray,
Ere thy season pass away;
Ere He set His judgment throne;
Ere the day of grace be gone.

Christ is earnest, bids thee come;
Paid thy spirit's priceless sum;
Wilt thou spurn thy Saviour's love,
Pleading with thee from above?

O be earnest, do not stay;
Thou mayest perish e'en to-day.
Rise, thou lost one, rise and flee;
Lo! thy Saviour waits for thee.

TUNE — "CYPRUS," ALSO CALLED "SHERBORNE."

## 89 — COME, YE SINNERS, POOR AND WRETCHED.

HYMNS, say some purists, ought only to be addressed to God. They may be right in the abstract, but, as a practical fact, hymns which are addressed to the congregation are often most useful. Their utility can sometimes be measured, which is impossible in the case where the hymn is addressed to the Deity. One of these hymns which these purists would drive from the hymn-book still retains its hold on the Christian Church. It was written by one of Whitfield's converts named Joseph Hart, who is still so far from being forgotten that an obelisk was erected over his grave in Bunhill Fields so recently as 1875. It is in great use at revival services, and has been cut about extensively to suit the views of the different gospellers.

COME, ye sinners, poor and wretched,
    Weak and wounded, sick and sore,
Jesus ready stands to save you,
    Full of pity joined with power;
        He is able,
    He is willing: doubt no more.

Come, ye needy, come and welcome,
    God's free bounty glorify;
True belief, and true repentance,
    Every grace that brings us nigh,
        Without money,
    Come to Jesus Christ and buy.

Let not conscience make you linger,
    Nor of fitness fondly dream;
All the fitness He requireth,
    Is to feel your need of Him:
        This He gives you;
    'T is the Spirit's rising beam.

Come, ye weary, heavy laden,
　Bruised and broken by the fall;
If you tarry till you're better,
　You will never come at all.
　　Not the righteous,
　Sinners, Jesus came to call.

Agonising in the garden,
　Lo! your Saviour prostrate lies:
On the bloody tree behold Him;
　Hear Him cry before He dies,—
　　It is finished!
　Finished the great sacrifice.

Lo! the Incarnate God, ascended,
　Pleads the merit of His blood.
Venture on Him, venture wholly,
　Let no other trust intrude:
　　None but Jesus
　Can do helpless sinners good.

Saints and angels joined in concert,
　Sing the praises of the Lamb:
While the blissful seats of heaven
　Sweetly echo with His name.
　　Hallelujah!
　Sinners here may sing the same.

　　　　　　　TUNE — "COMMUNION."

# XII.—Joy, Love, and Peace.

## 90—OUR GOD, OUR HELP IN AGES PAST.

MR. ASQUITH, late Home Secretary, writes: "My favourite among hymns is, and has for a long time been, Watts's 'Our God, our Help in Ages past.' I feel sure that your collection when complete will be both interesting and useful."

Watts wrote this as a paraphrase of the Ninetieth Psalm, a psalm which, as Mr. Marson reminds us, has been sung or read over the graves of our fathers ever since 1662. Burns paraphrased this psalm and failed, although he delighted in it greatly. Charles V. used to declare he preferred this to all other psalms, and Cardinal Newman makes Gerontius hear the souls in purgatory singing this psalm. The first four verses of this psalm form the burial-song of the Russian Church. It was chanted as a dirge at the funeral of John Hampden.

OUR God, our help in ages past,
    Our hope for years to come,
Our shelter from the stormy blast,
    And our eternal home;

Under the shadow of Thy throne
    Thy saints have dwelt secure;
Sufficient is Thine arm alone,
    And our defence is sure.

Before the hills in order stood,
    Or earth received her frame;
From everlasting Thou art God,
    To endless years the same.

A thousand ages in Thy sight
    Are like an evening gone;
Short as the watch that ends the night
    Before the rising sun.

The busy tribes of flesh and blood,
    With all their cares and fears,
Are carried downwards by the flood,
    And lost in following years.

Time, like an ever-rolling stream,
    Bears all its sons away;
They fly, forgotten, as a dream
    Dies at the opening day.

Our God, our help in ages past,
　Our hope for years to come,
Be Thou our guard, while troubles last
　And our eternal home.

　　　　　　　　　　　Tune — "St. Anne."

The Right Hon. Sir Henry Fowler writes to me: "John Bright used to speak in the highest terms of the grand hymn, 'Our God, our Help in Ages past.' I once told Dr. Liddon that Mr. Bright had described that hymn as the best in the language. Dr. Liddon paused, and then said: 'I should not say *the* best, but one of the three best.'"

## 91 — O GOD OF BETHEL, BY WHOSE HAND.

When I asked the Duke of Argyll as to hymns which had helped him, he made the following reference to Dr. Doddridge's well-known paraphrase: —

　　　　　　　Inverary, Argyllshire.

Sir, — I would be very glad to help you if I could, but I can't honestly say that any one hymn has "helped" me specially. Some of the Scotch paraphrases are my favourites, "O God of Bethel," etc.

　　　Yours obediently,　　　　Argyll.

O GOD of Bethel, by whose hand
　　Thy people still are fed;
Who through this weary pilgrimage
　Hast all our fathers led;

Our vows, our prayers, we now present
　Before Thy throne of grace;
God of our fathers, be the God
　Of their succeeding race.

Through each perplexing path of life
  Our wandering footsteps guide;
Give us, each day, our daily bread,
  And raiment fit provide.

O spread Thy covering wings around,
  Till all our wanderings cease,
And at our Father's loved abode,
  Our souls arrive in peace.

Such blessings from Thy gracious hand
  Our humble prayers implore;
And Thou shalt be our chosen God
  And portion, evermore.

                    TUNE — "FARRANT."

Of this hymn and the way it has helped men, Mr. S. R. Crockett writes as follows: "One hymn I love, and that (to be Irish) is not a hymn, but what in our country is mystically termed a 'paraphrase.' It is that which, when sung to the tune of St. Paul's, makes men and women square themselves and stand erect to sing, like an army that goes gladly to battle:—

    O God of Bethel, by whose hand
      Thy people still are fed:
    Who through this weary pilgrimage
      Hast all our fathers led.

"I wish I could quote it all. Of course it is in vain to try to tell what these songs of 'Christ's ain Kirk and Covenant' are to us who sucked them in with our mother-milk, and heard them crooned for cradle songs to 'Coleshill' and 'Kilmarnock.' But be assured that whatever new songs are written, noble and sincere, there will always be a number who will walk in the old paths, and, by choice, seek for their 'helping' (about which they will mostly keep silence) from the songs their fathers sang."

This was the favourite hymn of Dr. Livingstone. It cheered him often in his African wanderings, and when his remains were buried in Westminster Abbey it was sung over his grave.

A Scotch mission-teacher at Kuruman, Bechuanaland, South Africa, writes: "This hymn stands out preeminently as the hymn which has helped me beyond all others. It shines with radiant lustre like the star that outshineth all others among the midnight constellations. It has been my solace and comfort in times of trouble, my cheer in times of joy; it is woven into the warp and woof of my spiritual being; its strains were the first I was taught to lisp, and, God helping me, they shall be the last. Sung to the tune of 'Dundee,' that was the refrain of happy meetings or sad partings. Its strains rang out the Old Year and heralded the New. It was chanted as a farewell dirge when I left my home in Scotland. It has followed me 'Sooth the line,' and every gait I gang, I never rest until from dusky throats roll out the familiar words. It is a 'couthy' psalm, and touches to the quick the human spirit that more gifted utterances fail to reach. I am penning this in the little room that was once the study of David Livingstone, whose walls have often re-echoed to many a strain of praise and supplication, but to none more inspiring and endearing than 'O God of Bethel.'" Another Scotchman writes: "In some ways I have wandered far from the faith of our fathers, but the old Psalms move me strongly yet. 'O God of Bethel, by whose hand' will ever have a pathetic interest for me. I, too, have crooned it as a cradle song over one who will never need to hear me croon it ever more, for she has solved the riddle of the ages, which I am left painfully trying to spell. These rugged lines speak out the religious experiences of a rugged race as no modern hymns ever will."

## 92—NOW I HAVE FOUND THE GROUND WHEREIN.

THIS hymn is John Wesley's version of Rothe's "Ich habe nun den Grund gefunden." Rothe was Count Zinzendorf's friend and pastor at Berthelsdorf.

NOW I have found the ground wherein
  Sure my soul's anchor may remain:—
The wounds of Jesus, for my sin,
Before the world's foundation slain:
Whose mercy shall unshaken stay,
When heaven and earth are fled away.

O Love, thou bottomless abyss!
My sins are swallowed up in thee;
Covered is mine unrighteousness,
Nor spot of guilt remains on me,
While Jesus' blood, through earth and skies,
Mercy, free, boundless mercy cries!

With faith I plunge me in this sea:
Here is my hope, my joy, my rest!
Hither, when hell assails, I flee;
I look into my Saviour's breast;
Away, sad doubt, and anxious fear!
Mercy is all that's written there.

Though waves and storms go o'er my head,
Though strength, and health, and friends be gone,
Though joys be withered all and dead,
Though every comfort be withdrawn;
On this my steadfast soul relies:
Father, Thy mercy never dies.

Fixed on this ground will I remain,
Though my heart fail, and flesh decay;
This anchor shall my soul sustain,
When earth's foundations melt away;
Mercy's full power I then shall prove,
Loved with an everlasting love.

TUNE — "STELLA."

According to "Notes on the Methodist Hymn-Book," this hymn has helped multitudes. Few hymns are so full of Scripture truth and Scripture phraseology.

There are said to be no fewer than thirty-six texts which can be traced in its thirty lines.

The veteran Wesleyan minister, the Rev. Charles Garrett, of Liverpool, places this hymn in the forefront as one which has been his companion and comfort all through his life's journey.

## 93—JESUS, THE VERY THOUGHT OF THEE.

THERE are fifty stanzas of this hymn of St. Bernard, of which only four are given here. The fifth, in Latin, is not Bernard's. It has been in constant use for seven hundred years. No other poem, says Julian, in any language has furnished so many hymns of sterling worth and well-deserved popularity to English and American hymnody.

JESUS, the very thought of Thee
  With sweetness fills my breast;
But sweeter far Thy face to see,
  And in Thy presence rest.

Nor voice can sing, nor heart can frame,
  Nor can the memory find,
A sweeter sound than Thy blest name,
  O Saviour of mankind!

O hope of every contrite heart!
  O joy of all the meek!
To those who fall, how kind Thou art!
  How good to those who seek!

But what to those who find? Ah! this
  Nor tongue nor pen can show;
The love of Jesus — what it is,
  None but His loved ones know.

JESU dulcis memoria,
    Dans vera cordi gaudia:
Sed super mel et omnia
Ejus dulcis præsentia.

Nil canitur suavius,
Nil auditur jucundius,
Nil cogitatur dulcius,
Quam Jesus Dei Filius.

Jesu spes pœnitentibus,
Quam pius es petentibus!
Quam bonus te quærentibus!
Sed quid invenientibus!

Nec lingua valet dicere,
Nec littera exprimere;
Expertus potest credere,
Quid sit Jesum diligere.

Sis, Jesu, nostrum gaudium,
Qui es futurus præmium:
Sit nostra in te gloria,
Per cuncta semper sæcula.    Amen.

TUNE — "ST. AGNES."

## 94 — HOW SWEET THE NAME OF JESUS SOUNDS.

THIS is one of the most popular of Newton's hymns. The word Guardian in the fourth verse was originally written Husband, in allusion to the Church, "the Lamb's wife."

HOW sweet the name of Jesus sounds
    In a believer's ear!
It soothes his sorrows, heals his wounds,
    And drives away his fear.

It makes the wounded spirit whole,
　And calms the troubled breast:
'T is manna to the hungry soul,
　And to the weary, rest.

Dear name! the rock on which I build;
　My shield and hiding-place,
My never-failing treasury, filled
　With boundless stores of grace.

Jesus, my Shepherd, Guardian, Friend;
　My Prophet, Priest, and King;
My Lord, my life, my way, mine end,
　Accept the praise I bring.

Weak is the effort of my heart,
　And cold my warmest thought;
But when I see Thee as Thou art,
　I'll praise Thee as I ought:

Till then, I would Thy love proclaim
　With every fleeting breath;
And may the music of Thy name
　Refresh my soul in death.

　　　　　　　　TUNE — "ST. PETER."

## 95 — LOVE DIVINE, ALL LOVES EXCELLING.

THIS is one of the hymns of Charles Wesley, which enabled Methodism to sing itself into the heart of the human race.

LOVE divine, all loves excelling,
　Joy of heaven, to earth come down;
Fix in us Thy humble dwelling;
　All Thy faithful mercies crown.
Jesus, Thou art all compassion;
　Pure, unbounded love Thou art:
Visit us with Thy salvation;
　Enter every longing heart.

Come, almighty to deliver,
  Let us all Thy grace receive;
Suddenly return, and never,
  Never more Thy temples leave.
Thee we would be always blessing,
  Serve Thee as Thy hosts above;
Pray, and praise Thee without ceasing;
  Glory in Thy precious love.

Finish, then, Thy new creation;
  Pure, unspotted may we be:
Let us see our whole salvation
  Perfectly secured by Thee:
Changed from glory into glory,
  Till in heaven we take our place,
Till we cast our crowns before Thee!
  Lost in wonder, love, and praise.

                    TUNE — " BITHYNIA."

It is one of the most popular and helpful hymns, which, originating in the Methodist hymnody, have found an honoured place in the hymn-books of almost every other denomination. It was a prime favourite of Henry Ward Beecher. No one who ever heard the great congregation of Plymouth Church sing "Love Divine" is likely to forget the soul-stirring effect.

## 96—OH FOR A THOUSAND TONGUES TO SING.

THE first man whom this hymn helped was Charles Wesley himself. On May 21, 1738, Charles Wesley experienced that practical spiritual change which among Methodists is known as Conversion. Twelve months afterwards, in memory of a year in which he had found peace and joy in believing, he wrote the exultant outburst of grateful praise which, being given the first place in the Methodist hymn-book, may be said to strike the key-note of the whole of Methodism, that multitudinous chorus, whose voices, like the sound of many waters, encompass the world. The germ idea of the hymn was given to the author by Peter Bohler, the Moravian, who once declared: "Had I a thousand tongues I would praise Christ with them all." Originally, the exuberance of Wesley's gratitude overflowed into sixty-eight verses, only the best of which are used for singing. The third verse is an equal favourite of condemned malefactors and dying saints.

OH for a thousand tongues to sing
  My dear Redeemer's praise,
The glories of my God and King,
  The triumphs of His grace!

Jesus — the name that charms our fears,
  That bids our sorrows cease;
'T is music in the sinner's ears;
  'T is life, and health, and peace.

He breaks the power of cancelled sin,
  And sets the prisoner free:
His blood can make the foulest clean;
  His blood availed for me.

He speaks; and, listening to His voice,
  New life the dead receive;
The mournful broken hearts rejoice;
  The humble poor believe.

Hear Him, ye deaf; His praise, ye dumb,
  Your loosened tongues employ;
Ye blind, behold your Saviour come;
  And leap, ye lame, for joy!

My gracious Master and my God,
  Assist me to proclaim
And spread through all the earth abroad
  The honours of Thy name.

TUNE — "BYZANTIUM."

Mortimer Collins says: "Wesley's hymns are as much in earnest as Dibdin's sea-songs. I suspect Charles Wesley the poet did as much as John Wesley the orator for the permanence of Methodism. The magnetism of personal influence passes away; but the burning life of that wondrous psalmody, sung Sunday after Sunday by congregations full of faith, is imperishable."

## 97 — THOU HIDDEN LOVE OF GOD.

THERE is a peculiar interest attached to this hymn. John Wesley is said to have translated it in Savannah, in the United States, where he suffered much and was grievously tormented by his ill-starred passion for a certain Miss Sophy. It was with special reference to the continually obtruding thought of this Miss Sophy that the Rev. John composed the verse "Is there a thing beneath the sun?" It seems to have been efficacious, and the lovelorn poet came home to meet a worse fate at the hands of her whom, for his Karma, he was allowed to make Mrs. Wesley. The hymn has helped thousands who never knew of Wesley and his ill-fated loves to acts of consecration and self-sacrifice from which they would otherwise have shrunk. Tersteegen, the original author of the hymn "Verborgne Gottesliebe, Du," was a German mystical poet who died in 1769.

THOU hidden Love of God, whose height,
    Whose depth unfathomed, no man knows:
I see from far Thy bounteous light,
Inly I sigh for Thy repose:
My heart is pained, nor can it be
At rest, till it finds rest in Thee.

'T is mercy all, that Thou hast brought
My mind to seek her peace in Thee:
Yet while I seek, but find Thee not,

No peace my wandering soul shall see:
O when shall all my wanderings end,
And all my steps to Thee-ward tend!

Is there a thing beneath the sun
That strives with Thee my heart to share?
Ah! tear it thence, and reign alone,
The Lord of every motion there:
Then shall my heart from earth be free:
When it hath found repose in Thee.

O Love, Thy sovereign aid impart,
To save me from low-thoughted care:
Chase this self-will through all my heart,
Through all its latent mazes there:
Make me Thy duteous child, that I
Ceaseless may Abba, Father, cry!

Tune—"Rest" or "Euphony."

## 98—I HEARD THE VOICE OF JESUS.

This is one of the most popular of Dr. Bonar's hymns. It belongs to the number of those in which the converted recite their experiences for the encouragement of the unconverted. The persistent use of "I" and "me" in this hymn has helped it to help many to whom "we" and "us" would have been much less effective.

I HEARD the voice of Jesus say,
  "Come unto me and rest;
Lay down, thou weary one, lay down
  Thy head upon My breast."
I came to Jesus as I was,
  Weary and worn and sad,
I found in Him a resting-place,
  And He has made me glad.

I heard the voice of Jesus say,
  "Behold, I freely give

The living water; thirsty one,
  Stoop down and drink, and live."
I came to Jesus, and I drank
  Of that life-giving stream,
My thirst was quenched, my soul revived,
  And now I live in Him.

I heard the voice of Jesus say,
  " I am this dark world's light,
Look unto Me, thy morn shall rise,
  And all thy day be bright."
I looked to Jesus, and I found
  In Him my Star, my Sun;
And in that light of life I 'll walk,
  Till travelling days are done.

TUNE—"VOX DILECTI."

## 99—SAFE IN THE ARMS OF JESUS.

THIS little hymn by Mrs. Van Alstyne has comforted many, and will continue to do so. There are many souls from whom the craving for being "mothered" has been left out. To them the longing to be folded in loving arms and pressed to a tender and sympathetic bosom is unintelligible. But to those who never outgrow, even in their maturest years, when overwhelmed by affliction, the instinctive heart-longing to seek the sheltering arms which comforted them in their childhood, this hymn is a special and most helpful favourite. It is when people are hard hit they need help. The just need no repentance, and the happy need no helper. But for the miserable, the promise of the shelter of the Everlasting Arms is sweet.

SAFE in the arms of Jesus,
  Safe on His gentle breast,
There by His love o'ershaded,
  Sweetly my soul shall rest.

Hark! 't is the voice of angels
　Borne in a song to me,
Over the fields of glory,
　Over the jasper sea.
　　Safe in the arms of Jesus, safe on His
　　　gentle breast;
　　There by His love o'ershaded, sweetly
　　　my soul shall rest.

Safe in the arms of Jesus,
　Safe from corroding care,
Safe from the world's temptations,
　Sin cannot harm me there.
Free from the blight of sorrow,
　Free from my doubts and fears;
Only a few more trials, —
　Only a few more tears!

Jesus, my heart's dear Refuge,
　Jesus has died for me;
Firm on the Rock of Ages
　Ever my trust shall be.
Here let me wait with patience,
　Wait till the night is o'er;
Wait till I see the morning
　Break on the golden shore.

　　　　　Tune — From "Songs and Solos."

## 100 — O JESU, KING MOST WONDERFUL.

This is another part of St. Bernard's hymn, "Jesu dulcis memoria," which is noticed under the heading "Jesus, the very thought of Thee."

O JESU, King most wonderful,
　　Thou Conqueror renowned;
Thou sweetness most ineffable,
　In whom all joys are found; —

When once Thou visitest the heart,
  Then truth begins to shine,
Then earthly vanities depart,
  Then kindles love divine.

O Jesus, light of all below,
  Thou fount of life and fire,
Surpassing all the joys we know,
  All that we can desire;—

May every heart confess Thy name,
  And ever Thee adore:
And, seeking Thee, itself inflame
  To seek Thee more and more.

Thee may our tongues for ever bless,
  Thee may we love alone;
And ever in our lives express
  The image of Thine own.

TUNE—"ST. AGNES."

## 101—COME, THOU FOUNT OF EVERY BLESSING.

THIS hymn for a hundred years has been a great favourite. It has been wrongfully attributed to the Countess of Huntingdon. Its real author was one Robert Robinson, of whom a somewhat pathetic story is told. In his later years, this Robinson somewhat fell away from grace and displayed such levity in a stage-coach as to lead a lady fellow-passenger to labour with him in the Lord. As a final shot, she, all unknowing who the stranger was, quoted to him this hymn and spoke of how it had been blessed to her soul. Thereupon Robinson burst out into tears, crying: "Madam, I am the poor unhappy man who composed that hymn many years ago, and I would give a thousand worlds, if I had them, to enjoy the feelings I had then."

COME, Thou fount of every blessing,
  Tune my heart to sing Thy grace;
Streams of mercy, never ceasing,
  Call for songs of loudest praise:
Teach me some melodious sonnet
  Sung by flaming tongues above;
Praise the mount — I'm fixed upon it!
  Mount of Thy redeeming love!

Here I'll raise my Ebenezer,
  Hither by Thy help I've come;
And I hope, by Thy good pleasure,
  Safely to arrive at home.
Jesus sought me when a stranger,
  Wandering from the fold of God;
He, to rescue me from danger,
  Interposed His precious blood.

Oh, to grace how great a debtor
  Daily I'm constrained to be!
Let Thy grace, Lord, like a fetter,
  Bind my wandering heart to Thee.
Prone to wander, Lord, I feel it;
  Prone to leave the God I love;
Here's my heart, oh, take and seal it,
  Seal it for Thy courts above.
                TUNE — "NORMANDY."

## 102 — I NEED THEE EVERY HOUR.

THIS is a hymn by Mrs. A. S. Hawks which has been much used at missions, revival meetings, and the like.

I NEED Thee every hour, most gracious Lord:
  No tender voice like Thine can peace afford.
    I need Thee, oh, I need Thee; every hour
      I need Thee:
    Oh, bless me now, my Saviour! I come to
      Thee.

I need Thee every hour: stay Thou near by:
Temptations lose their power when Thou art nigh.

I need Thee every hour, in joy or pain;
Come quickly and abide, or life is vain.

I need Thee every hour: teach me Thy will;
And Thy rich promises in me fulfil.

I need Thee every hour, most Holy One;
Oh, make me Thine indeed, Thou blessed Son.
    TUNE — BY REV. R. LOWRY IN "SONGS AND SOLOS."

## 103 — O SACRED HEAD ONCE WOUNDED.

THIS is another of the "hymns that have helped" which we owe to St. Bernard of Clairvaux. Its genesis is direct. In Bernard's Rhythmica Oratio, Part vii. begins: "Salve caput cruentatum." Gerhardt published a German version in the seventeenth century, beginning: "O Haupt voll Blut und Wunden." Dr. Alexander, an American Presbyterian, translated it into English in 1830.

Dr. Philip Schaff says: "This classical hymn has shown in three tongues, Latin, German, and English, and in three Confessions, Roman, Lutheran, and Reformed, with equal effect, the dying love of our Saviour and our boundless indebtedness to Him."

O SACRED Head once wounded,
    With grief and pain weigh'd down,
How scornfully surrounded
    With thorns — Thine only crown!
How art Thou pale with anguish,
    With sore abuse and scorn!
How does that visage languish,
    Which once was bright as morn!

O Lord of life and glory,
    What bliss till now was Thine!

I read the wondrous story,
  I joy to call Thee mine.
Thy grief and Thy compassion
  Were all for sinners' gain;
Mine, mine was the transgression,
  But Thine the deadly pain.

What language shall I borrow
  To praise Thee, Heavenly Friend,
For this Thy dying sorrow,
  Thy pity without end?
Lord, make me Thine for ever,
  Nor let me faithless prove;
Oh, let me never, never
  Abuse such dying love.

Be near me, Lord, when dying;
  Oh, show Thy cross to me;
And, for my succour flying,
  Come, Lord, to set me free:
These eyes, new faith receiving,
  From Jesus shall not move;
For he who dies believing,
  Dies safely through Thy love.

                  TUNE — "PASSION CHORALE."

## 104—JESUS, AND SHALL IT EVER BE.

THIS hymn dates from the middle of last century. There are several hymns like it intended to encourage the diffident believer to profess his faith. "Ashamed to be a Christian" is another of the same kind. They are more practical than many much more admired hymns. Its author was one Joseph Gregg; the original poem, entitled "Glorying in Jesus," contained seven stanzas.

JESUS, and shall it ever be,
    A mortal man ashamed of Thee?
Scorned be the thought by rich and poor:
My soul shall scorn it more and more.

Ashamed of Jesus! Sooner far
May evening blush to own a star.
Ashamed of Jesus! Just as soon
May midnight blush to think of noon.

Ashamed of Jesus! that dear Friend,
On whom my hopes of heaven depend?
No! when I blush, be this my shame,
That I no more revere His name.

Ashamed of Jesus! Yes, I may,
When I've no sins to wash away,
No tears to wipe, no joys to crave,
No fears to quell, no soul to save.

Till then — nor is the boasting vain —
Till then I boast a Saviour slain:
And Oh, may this my glory be,
That Christ is not ashamed of me.

                TUNE — "BROOKFIELD."

## 105 — MUST JESUS BEAR THE CROSS ALONE.

A STIRRING hymn with a spirited tune, it is associated, in the minds of many, with the turning-point of their life. It is a great favourite with the Salvation Army, which has gathered in many of its converts to its strains.

MUST Jesus bear the Cross alone,
    And all the world go free?
No, there's a Cross for everyone,
    And there's a Cross for me.

If the Cross we boldly bear
Then the crown we shall wear,
When we dwell with Jesus there
In the bright forevermore.

The consecrated Cross I'll bear
  Till death shall set me free,
And then go home my crown to wear,
  For there's a crown for me.

Upon the crystal pavement, down
  At Jesus' piercèd feet,
Joyful I'll cast my golden crown,
  And His dear name repeat.

TUNE FROM SALVATION ARMY BOOK.

## 106—IN THE CROSS OF CHRIST I GLORY.

SIR JOHN BOWRING, LL.D., F.R.S., was a Unitarian who, in his day, played a rather important part in our Chinese wars. He was a polyglot scholar, a Radical M.P., Consul at Hong Kong when the Opium War broke out, and afterwards Governor of that Colony. He was the author of several hymns, of which this is the best known and most used. Its first line is inscribed on his tombstone.

IN the Cross of Christ I glory;
  Towering o'er the wrecks of time,
All the light of sacred story
  Gathers round its head sublime.

When the woes of life o'ertake me,
  Hopes deceive, and fears annoy,
Never shall the Cross forsake me:
  Lo! it glows with peace and joy.

When the sun of bliss is beaming
  Light and love upon my way:

From the Cross the radiance streaming
  Adds more lustre to the day.

Bane and blessing, pain and pleasure,
  By the Cross are sanctified;
Peace is there, that knows no measure,
  Joys, that through all time abide.

In the Cross of Christ I glory;
  Towering o'er the wrecks of time,
All the light of sacred story
  Gathers round its head sublime.

TUNE — " SARDIS."

## 107 — PEACE, PERFECT PEACE.

"BICKERSTETH'S 'Peace, perfect peace,'" writes Richard Le Gallienne, "comes very near 'Lead, Kindly Light,' in combining piety and poetry in the highest proportion. But, after all, that hymn is best which sings best rather than reads best, which best lends itself to the breath of devotion vibrating through it as through an instrument." Bishop Bickersteth wrote it in 1875, on the text, "Thou will keep him in perfect peace whose mind is stayed on Thee, because he trusteth in Thee."

PEACE, perfect peace, in this dark world of sin?
  The blood of Jesus whispers peace within.

Peace, perfect peace, by thronging duties pressed?
To do the will of Jesus, this is rest.

Peace, perfect peace, with sorrows surging round?
On Jesus' bosom nought but calm is found.

Peace, perfect peace, with loved ones far away?
In Jesus' keeping we are safe, and they.

Peace, perfect peace, our future all unknown?
Jesus we know, and He is on the throne.

Peace, perfect peace, death shadowing us and
 ours?
Jesus has vanquish'd death and all its powers.

It is enough: earth's struggles soon shall cease,
And Jesus call us to Heav'n's perfect peace.

TUNE—"PAX TECUM."

# XIII.—Morning and Evening.

## 108—AWAKE, MY SOUL, AND WITH THE SUN.

AWAKE, my soul, and with the sun
Thy daily stage of duty run:
Shake off dull sloth, and joyful rise
To pay thy morning sacrifice.

Thy precious time, misspent, redeem;
Each present day, thy last esteem;
Improve thy talent with due care;
For the Great Day thyself prepare.

In conversation be sincere;
Keep conscience as the noontide clear.
Think how All-seeing God thy ways,
Thy every secret thought surveys.

Wake, and lift up thyself, my heart,
And with the angels bear thy part,
Who, all night long, unwearied sing
High praise to the Eternal King.

All praise to Thee, who safe has kept,
And hast refreshed me while I slept.
Grant, Lord, when I from death shall wake,
I may of endless life partake.

Lord, I my vows to Thee renew:
Scatter my sins as morning dew:
Guard my first springs of thought and will,
And with Thyself my spirit fill.

Direct, control, suggest, this day,
All I design, or do, or say;
That all my powers, with all their might,
In Thy sole glory may unite.

Praise God from whom all blessings flow:
Praise Him all creatures here below:
Praise Him above, ye heavenly host:
Praise Father, Son, and Holy Ghost.

      TUNE — "MORNING HYMN."

Bishop Ken, the author of this hymn, led a rather troubled and eventful life. He bore stern testimony against the immorality of the Restoration, refusing to admit Nell Gwynne to his house; but he was called in to attend the death-bed of Charles the Second when that merry monarch was "such an unconscionable time in dying." He was sent to the Tower by James along with the other bishops who would not publish the Declaration of Indulgence. But when William came he refused to swear allegiance, and died a non-juror in 1711. He used to sing this morning hymn to his own accompaniment on the lute, and when he died he was buried under the east window of the chancel of Frome Church, just at sunrising, as his mourning friends sang, in the first light of the dawning day, " Awake, my soul, and with the sun." Macaulay says of him that his character approached as near as human infirmity permits to the ideal perfection of Christian virtue. Monckton Milnes wrote a hymn upon his grave, styling him

  "A braver Becket — who could hope
   To conquer unresisting."

If it was for nothing else, this hymn is famous as a help because its last verse has become the universal doxology of the English-speaking world,—a kind of pious pemmican of devotion not unworthy to be sung wherever the Lord's Prayer is prayed. Mr. Thomas Hardy, author of "Tess" and other novels, places this among the three hymns he loves most.

### 109.—CARLYLE'S MORNING HYMN.

VERY different from Bishop Ken's, but, nevertheless, not without helpfulness of its own, is Thomas Carlyle's charming little hymn for the dawning of the morning.

SO here hath been dawning
　　Another blue day;
Think, wilt thou let it
　　Slip useless away?

Out of eternity
　　This new day is born;
Into eternity
　　At night will return.

Behold it aforetime
　　No eye ever did;
So soon it for ever
　　From all eyes is hid.

Here hath been dawning
　　Another blue day;
Think, wilt thou let it
　　Slip useless away?

### 110—O TIMELY HAPPY, TIMELY WISE.

"THIS morning hymn of Keble's from the *Christian Year* has been to me," says a correspondent in Brisbane, "more helpful than anything else I ever read." The sixth verse is the kernel of the hymn.

O TIMELY happy, timely wise,
   Hearts that with rising morn arise;
Eyes that the beam celestial view,
Which evermore makes all things new.

New every morning is the love
Our wakening and uprising prove;
Through sleep and darkness safely brought,
Restored to life and power and thought.

New mercies, each returning day,
Hover around us while we pray;
New perils past, new sins forgiven,
New thoughts of God, new hopes of heaven.

If on our daily course our mind
Be set to hallow all we find,
New treasures still, of countless price,
God will provide for sacrifice.

Old friends, old scenes, will lovelier be,
As more of heaven in each we see;
Some softening gleam of love and prayer
Shall dawn on every cross and care.

The trivial round, the common task,
Will furnish all we ought to ask:
Room to deny ourselves; a road
To bring us daily nearer God.

Only, O Lord, in Thy dear love,
Fit us for perfect rest above;
And help us, this and every day,
To live more nearly as we pray.

TUNE — "NICOMACHUS."

Another correspondent sends me this hymn as one which she has never called to mind without its proving of great help in assisting her to build up more than one Christian virtue. In the United States the hymn begins, in most churches, with the second stanza.

## 111 — SUN OF MY SOUL.

KEBLE's evening hymn has far outstripped in general use his morning hymn. Although the *Christian Year* has gone through one hundred editions, the last of which placed the bulk of it before one hundred thousand readers, this hymn is known not to thousands, but to millions, and the music of its verse is familiar in every nook and corner of the English-speaking world.

SUN of my soul, Thou Saviour dear!
It is not night, if Thou be near;
O may no earth-born cloud arise,
To hide Thee from Thy servant's eyes!

When with dear friends sweet talk I hold,
And all the flowers of life unfold,
Let not my heart within me burn
Except in all I Thee discern.

When the soft dews of kindly sleep
My weary eyelids gently steep,
Be my last thought, how sweet to rest
For ever on my Saviour's breast!

Abide with me from morn till eve,
For without Thee I cannot live:
Abide with me when night is nigh,
For without Thee I dare not die.

Thou Framer of the light and dark,
Steer through the tempest Thine own ark:
Amid the howling wintry sea,
We are in port if we have Thee.

If some poor wandering child of Thine
Have spurned, to-day, the voice divine,
Now, Lord, the gracious work begin;
Let him no more lie down in sin.

Watch by the sick: enrich the poor
With blessings from Thy boundless store:
Be every mourner's sleep to-night,
Like infants' slumbers, pure and light.

Come near and bless us when we wake,
Ere through the world our way we take:
Till in the ocean of Thy love
We lose ourselves in heaven above.

TUNE—"HURSLEY."

## 112—ABIDE WITH ME.

THIS was the Swan Song of the Rev. H. F. Lyte. He produced it on the evening of the Sunday on which he preached his last sermon. It is generally used as an evening hymn. It was not so intended. It refers to the evening of life, not of the day, and is more of a hymn for the dying than for those about to renew their strength by a night's rest. It was sung at the burial of Professor Maurice, and is in constant use throughout the English-speaking world. Lyte is buried in Nice, and his grave is still sometimes sought out by pilgrims from far across the seas who attribute their conversion to this hymn.

ABIDE with me, fast falls the eventide:
  The darkness thickens: Lord, with me abide;
When other helpers fail, and comforts flee,
Help of the helpless, Oh abide with me.

Swift to its close ebbs out life's little day;
Earth's joys grow dim, its glories pass away;
Change and decay in all around I see:
O Thou who changest not, abide with me.

Not a brief glance I beg, a passing word,
But as Thou dwell'st with Thy disciples, Lord,—
Familiar, condescending, patient, free,—
Come not to sojourn, but abide with me.

Come not in terrors, as the King of kings,
But kind and good, with healing in Thy wings;
Tears for all woes, a heart for every plea;
Come, Friend of sinners, thus abide with me.

I need Thy presence every passing hour;
What but Thy grace can foil the tempter's power?
Who like Thyself my guide and stay can be?
Through cloud and sunshine, O abide with me.

I fear no foe, with Thee at hand to bless,
Ills have no weight, and tears no bitterness.
Where is Death's sting? where, Grave, thy victory?
I triumph still, if Thou abide with me.

Hold Thou Thy cross before my closing eyes,
Shine through the gloom, and point me to the skies:
Heaven's morning breaks, and earth's vain shadows flee;
In life, in death, O Lord, abide with me.

TUNE—"EVENTIDE."

Mrs. Mona Caird's three favourite hymns are, " Lead, Kindly Light," " As pants the Hart," and " Abide with me." " These three," she says, " possess for me the stay and power of succour. They seem to refer me back to the great unknown in which and in whom all of us believe, whatever name we may give to our divinity."

## 113—AT EVEN, ERE THE SUN WAS SET.

EVENING hymns are much more popular than those for morning use. And among evening hymns few are better known or more used than this, written by Canon Twells in 1868.

AT even, ere the sun was set,
    The sick, O Lord, around Thee lay;
O in what divers pains they met!
    O with what joy they went away!

Once more 't is eventide, and we,
    Oppressed with various ills, draw near.
What if thy form we cannot see?
    We know and feel that Thou art here.

O Saviour Christ, our woes dispel;
    For some are sick and some are sad;
And some have never loved Thee well,
    And some have lost the love they had.

And some are pressed with worldly care,
    And some are tried with sinful doubt;
And some such grievous passions tear
    That only Thou canst cast them out.

And some have found the world is vain,
    Yet from the world they break not free;
And some have friends who give them pain,
    Yet have not sought a friend in Thee.

And none, O Lord, have perfect rest,
    For none are wholly free from sin;
And they who fain would serve Thee best,
    Are conscious most of wrong within.

O Saviour Christ, Thou too art man;
    Thou hast been troubled, tempted, tried;
Thy kind but searching glance can scan
    The very wounds that shame would hide:

Thy touch has still its ancient power;
  No word from Thee can fruitless fall;
Hear in this solemn evening hour,
  And in thy mercy heal us all.

TUNE — "ANGELUS."

William Johnston, M.P., the well-known Orange leader, said: "No hymn now touches me more than that pathetic one, 'At Even, ere the Sun was set;' the verse beginning, 'O Saviour Christ' would be too painful but for the Healer's power."

## 114 — SAVIOUR, AGAIN TO THY DEAR NAME.

THIS evening hymn is the most popular of all the hymns of the Rev. John Ellerton. He wrote it for a festival of parochial choirs in Nantwich in 1866, and in less than thirty years it has sung its way around the world.

SAVIOUR, again to Thy dear name we raise
  With one accord our parting hymn of praise;
We stand to bless Thee ere our worship cease,
Then, lowly kneeling, wait Thy word of peace.

Grant us Thy peace through this approaching night;
Turn Thou for us its darkness into light;
From harm and danger keep Thy children free,
For dark and light are both alike to Thee.

Grant us Thy peace upon our homeward way;
With Thee began, with Thee shall end the day;
Guard Thou the lips from sin, the hearts from shame,
That in this house have call'd upon Thy name.

Grant us Thy peace throughout our earthly life,
Our balm in sorrow, and our stay in strife;
Then, when Thy voice shall bid our conflict cease,
Call us, O Lord, to Thine eternal peace.

TUNE—"PAX DEI."

## 115—SWEET SAVIOUR, BLESS US ERE WE GO.

THIS is Faber's evening hymn. Faber published it in 1852, six years after he quitted the English for the Roman Church.

SWEET Saviour, bless us ere we go;
   Thy word into our minds instil;
And make our lukewarm hearts to glow
   With lowly love and fervent will.
Through life's long day and death's dark night,
O gentle Jesus, be our light.

Grant us, dear Lord, from evil ways
   True absolution and release;
And bless us more than in past days
   With purity and inward peace.
Through life's long day and death's dark night,
O gentle Jesus, be our light.

Do more than pardon; give us joy,
   Sweet fear and sober liberty;
And loving hearts without alloy,
   That only long to be like thee.
Through life's long day and death's dark night,
O gentle Jesus, be our light.

Labour is sweet, for thou hast toiled;
   And care is light, for thou hast cared;
Let not our works with self be soiled,
   Nor in unsimple ways insnared.

Through life's long day and death's dark night,
O gentle Jesus, be our light.

For all we love — the poor, the sad,
   The sinful — unto thee we call;
Oh let thy mercy make us glad;
   Thou art our Jesus and our all.
Through life's long day and death's dark night,
O gentle Jesus, be our light.

                         TUNE — "ST. MATTHIAS."

It was written for use as the evening hymn at the Brompton Oratory. The last verse, omitted from Protestant hymn-books, is as follows:—

Sweet Saviour! bless us; night is come.
   Mary and Philip near us be.
Good angels watch about our home,
   May we each day be nearer Thee.
Through life's long day and death's dark night,
O gentle Jesus, be our light.

Philip was St. Philip Neri. In Catholic hymn-books he is usually superseded by Joseph.

## 116 — SAVIOUR, BREATHE AN EVENING BLESSING.

THIS hymn is one of the few which we owe indirectly to the somewhat savage Christianity of Abyssinia. Dr. Edmeston, its author, was so much impressed by reading an account by a traveller in Abyssinia of how at night the short evening hymn of the Abyssinian, "Jesus Mahaxaroo," "Jesus, forgive us," stole through the camp, that he composed this hymn, which has since been accepted everywhere as one of the best evening hymns in the language.

SAVIOUR, breathe an evening blessing,
   Ere repose our spirits seal;

Sin and want we come confessing:
 Thou canst save and Thou canst heal.
Though destruction walk around us,
 Though the arrows past us fly,
Angel-guards from Thee surround us;
 We are safe if Thou art nigh.

Though the night be dark and dreary,
 Darkness cannot hide from Thee;
Thou art He, who, never weary,
 Watchest where Thy people be.
Should swift death this night o'ertake us,
 And our couch become our tomb,
May the morn in heaven awake us,
 Clad in light and deathless bloom.

TUNE — "FLORENCE."

## 117 — GLORY TO THEE, MY GOD, THIS NIGHT.

THIS is Bishop Ken's evening hymn, — a hymn the music of which has become the common slumber-song of the English-speaking race.

GLORY to Thee, my God, this night,
 For all the blessings of the light.
Keep me, O keep me, King of kings,
Beneath Thine own almighty wings.

Forgive me, Lord, for Thy dear Son,
The ill that I this day have done;
That with the world, myself, and Thee,
I, ere I sleep, at peace may be.

Teach me to live, that I may dread,
The grave as little as my bed:
Teach me to die, that so I may
Rise glorious at the judgment-day.

Oh may my soul on Thee repose,
And with sweet sleep mine eyelids close; —
Sleep that may me more vigorous make,
To serve my God when I awake.

When in the night I sleepless lie,
My soul with heavenly thoughts supply;
Let no ill dreams disturb my rest,
No powers of darkness me molest.

Oh! when shall I in endless day,
For ever chase dark sleep away,
And hymns with the supernal choir
Incessant sing, and never tire?

Praise God from whom all blessings flow:
Praise Him, all creatures here below:
Praise Him above, ye heavenly host:
Praise Father, Son, and Holy Ghost.

TUNE — "CANON" BY TALLIS.

Archdeacon Sinclair, writing on this hymn, which he often repeats to himself the last thing before going to sleep, says that "Its majesty, simplicity, and ring of truth are unequalled. To live in the spirit of this hymn would be the ideal of Christian life."

# XIV.—Work.

## 118—A CHARGE TO KEEP I HAVE.

THE last line of this familiar hymn offends some people. But it can be used without difficulty even by those who are most in revolt against the doctrine of eternal punishment. At the same time, there is something so grim in singing even the sentence of doom that I would have left it out had the hymn not helped so many that it must stay in.

## HYMNS THAT HAVE HELPED. 215

A CHARGE to keep I have,
   A God to glorify;
A never-dying soul to save,
   And fit it for the sky;
To serve the present age,
   My calling to fulfil; —
O may it all my powers engage
   To do my Master's will.

Arm me with jealous care,
   As in Thy sight to live;
And Oh! Thy servant, Lord, prepare
   A strict account to give:
Help me to watch and pray,
   And on Thyself rely,
Assured, if I my trust betray,
   I shall for ever die.

TUNE — "VIGIL."

The Rev. Thomas Richardson, vicar of St. Benet's, Mile End Road, who founded the Bible and Prayer Union, which has now 334,000 enrolled members in every part of the world, says that this hymn has been the creed of his Christian life and active work for the past thirty-four years.

## 119 — LONGFELLOW'S PSALM OF LIFE.

THIS does not properly rank as a hymn, and although it is called a psalm, it figures in very few collections of sacred song. Sir Edwin Arnold, however, says it is one of the hymns that helped him, and as others have expressed a similar opinion, I give it a place.

TELL me not, in mournful numbers,
   "Life is but an empty dream!"
For the soul is dead that slumbers,
   And things are not what they seem.

Life is real! life is earnest!
   And the grave is not its goal;
"Dust thou art, to dust returnest,"
   Was not spoken of the soul.

Not enjoyment and not sorrow,
   Is our destined end or way;
But to act, that each to-morrow
   Find us farther than to-day.

Art is long, and time is fleeting,
   And our hearts, though stout and brave,
Still, like muffled drums, are beating
   Funeral marches to the grave.

In the world's broad field of battle,
   In the bivouac of life,
Be not like dumb, driven cattle, —
   Be a hero in the strife!

Trust no future, howe'er pleasant!
   Let the dead Past bury its dead!
Act, — act in the living Present,
   Heart within and God o'erhead!

Lives of great men all remind us;
   We can make *our* lives sublime
And, departing, leave behind us
   Footprints on the sands of time.

The proprietor of the *South Wales Gazette* maintains that the "Psalm of Life" is "singularly suitable for congregational singing, and has been helpful to many a soul assailed by the twin forces of pessimism and despair." Of this poem Sir Edwin Arnold says: "I have liked and lived by Longfellow's 'Psalm of Life.'" Mr. Harry Furniss says that Longfellow's "Psalm of Life" is to him the best of hymns, and "I must acknowledge that I frequently repeated the stanza 'Let us, then, be

HYMNS THAT HAVE HELPED. 217

up and doing' in my early days." He adds: "I do not know whether this comes in the category of hymns, but if it does not, it ought to." The Rev. Samuel Longfellow, brother of Henry, wrote several hymns which the Rev. Minot J. Savage says the Unitarians in the United States find exceedingly helpful.

## 120 — GOETHE'S "OHNE HAST UND OHNE RAST."

GOETHE's hymn I have taken from "Hymns and Anthems" used at the South Place Chapel. I would have liked to include the verses which Mr. Morley said came nearer expressing his ultimate thought than anything else, but I could not drag them even into my very wide net. So I content myself with this.

WITHOUT haste and without rest:
Bind the motto to thy breast,
Bear it with thee as a spell;
Storm or sunshine, guard it well!
Heed not flowers that round thee bloom;
Bear it onward to the tomb!

Haste not — let no thoughtless deed
Mar the spirit's steady speed;
Ponder well and know the right,
Onward then with all thy might;
Haste not — years can ne'er atone
For one reckless action done!

Rest not — life is sweeping by,
Do and dare before you die;
Something worthy and sublime
Leave behind to conquer time:
Glorious 't is to live for aye,
When these forms have passed away.

Haste not — rest not, calm in strife
Meekly bear the storms of life;
Duty be thy polar guide,
Do the right whate'er betide;
Haste not — rest not — conflicts past,
God shall crown thy work at last!

## 121 — WORKMAN OF GOD, O LOSE NOT HEART.

This — another contribution of Faber's to the hymnody of the Church Universal — is " As lofty as the love of God, and wide as are the wants of men."

WORKMAN of God, O lose not heart,
   But learn what God is like;
And in the darkest battle-field
   Thou shalt know where to strike.

Thrice blest is he to whom is given
   The instinct that can tell
That God is on the field when He
   Is most invisible.

Blest too is he who can divine
   Where real right doth lie,
And dares to take the side that seems
   Wrong to man's blindfold eye.

God's glory is a wondrous thing,
   Most strange in all its ways;
And, of all things on earth, least like
   What men agree to praise.

Muse on His justice, downcast soul,
   Muse, and take better heart;
Back with thine angel to the field,
   And bravely do thy part.

For right is right, since God is God;
  And right the day must win;
To doubt would be disloyalty,
  To falter would be sin.

## 122 — WORK, FOR THE NIGHT IS COMING.

YEARS ago, when the Darlington School Board was wrestling with the religious difficulties, a local disciple of Mr. Bradlaugh subjected Sankey's hymns to a critical examination, with the result that this hymn, " Work, for the night is coming," was declared to be the only hymn in the book that could be used in the Board Schools without giving offence to the Secularist conscience.

WORK, for the night is coming!
  Work through the morning hours;
Work while the dew is sparkling,
  Work 'mid springing flowers:
Work when the day grows brighter,
  Work in the glowing sun;
Work, for the night is coming,
  When man's work is done.

Work, for the night is coming,
  Work through the sunny noon:
Fill brightest hours with labour,
  Rest comes sure and soon.
Give every flying minute
  Something to keep in store:
Work, for the night is coming,
  When man works no more.

Work, for the night is coming,
  Under the sunset skies!
While their bright tints are glowing
  Work, for daylight flies.

Work till the last beam fadeth,
　Fadeth to shine no more :
Work while the night is dark'ning,
　When man's work is o'er.
　　　　Tune from "Songs and Solos."

## 123 — COURAGE, BROTHER! DO NOT STUMBLE.

This cheery marching song by the late Dr. Norman Macleod has a lilt and a go in it which are quite sufficient to explain its popularity. It is also free from any objection as to sectarian bias.

Courage, brother! do not stumble,
　Though thy path be dark as night;
There's a star to guide the humble; —
　Trust in God, and do the right.

Let the road be rough and dreary,
　And its end far out of sight,
Foot it bravely! strong or weary,
　Trust in God, and do the right.

Perish policy and cunning,
　Perish all that fears the light!
Whether losing, whether winning,
　Trust in God, and do the right.

Trust no party, sect, or faction;
　Trust no leaders in the fight;
But in every word and action
　Trust in God, and do the right.

Trust no lovely forms of passion, —
　Fiends may look like angels bright;
Trust no custom, school, or fashion —
　Trust in God, and do the right.

Simple rule, and safest guiding,
  Inward peace, and inward might,
Star upon our path abiding, —
  Trust in God, and do the right.

Some will hate thee, some will love thee,
  Some will flatter, some will slight;
Cease from man, and look above thee, —
  Trust in God, and do the right.

TUNE — "ST. OSWALD."

## 124 — STANDING BY A PURPOSE TRUE.

THIS little hymn, by Philip Bliss, Edna Lyall specially mentioned as one which had helped her. It is quaint, but it has helped many another to learn the lesson which is perhaps of all others most difficult to learn.

STANDING by a purpose true,
  Heeding God's command,
Honour them, the faithful few!
  All hail to Daniel's Band!
    Dare to be a Daniel! Dare to stand alone!
    Dare to have a purpose firm! Dare to make it known!

Many mighty men are lost,
  Daring not to stand,
Who for God had been a host,
  By joining Daniel's Band.

Many giants, great and tall,
  Stalking through the land,
Headlong to the earth would fall,
  If met by Daniel's Band!

    Hold the gospel banner high!
      On to victory grand!
    Satan and his host defy,
      And shout for Daniel's Band!
            TUNE FROM "SONGS AND SOLOS."

Edna Lyall wrote: "I can certainly say that the refrain of 'Dare to be a Daniel' has helped me again and again. I do not know the rest of the hymn well, and some of it is rather funny, still I think it ought to be in the hymn-book."

## 125 — RESCUE THE PERISHING.

IN 1885, in the outburst of public feeling that followed the publication of *The Maiden Tribute*, "Rescue the Perishing" was the hymn that was always sung at every public meeting in connection with that agitation.

RESCUE the perishing, care for the dying —
    Snatch them in pity from sin and the grave;
Weep o'er the erring one, lift up the fallen —
    Tell them of Jesus, the mighty to save.
      Rescue the perishing, care for the dying —
      Jesus is merciful, Jesus will save.

Though they are slighting Him, still He is waiting —
    Waiting the penitent child to receive.
Plead with them earnestly, plead with them gently:
    He will forgive if they only believe.

Down in the human heart, crushed by the tempter,
    Feelings lie buried that grace can restore;
Touched by a loving heart, wakened by kindness,
    Chords that were broken will vibrate once more.

Rescue the perishing — duty demands it;
　Strength for thy labour the Lord will provide;
Back to the narrow way patiently win them;
　Tell the poor wanderer a Saviour has died.

　　　　　　　TUNE FROM "SONGS AND SOLOS."

## 126 — SOWING THE SEED.

THIS hymn is from Sankey's collection, but, despite the criticism quoted on Hymn 122, it could surely be used by any assemblage that admitted the moral responsibility of man.

SOWING the seed by the dawn-light fair,
　Sowing the seed by the noonday glare,
Sowing the seed by the fading light,
Sowing the seed in the solemn night:
　Oh, what shall the harvest be?
　Oh, what shall the harvest be?

Sown in the darkness or sown in the light,
Sown in our weakness or sown in our might;
Gathered in time or eternity,
Sure, ah! sure, will the harvest be!

Sowing the seed by the wayside high,
Sowing the seed on the rocks to die;
Sowing the seed where the thorns will spoil,
Sowing the seed in the fertile soil:
　Oh, what shall the harvest be?

Sowing the seed of a ling'ring pain,
Sowing the seed of a maddened brain,
Sowing the seed of a tarnished name,
Sowing the seed of eternal shame:
　Oh, what shall the harvest be?

Sowing the seed with an aching heart,
Sowing the seed while the tear-drops start,

Sowing in hope till the reapers come
Gladly to gather the harvest home:
Oh, what shall the harvest be?

TUNE BY MR. BLISS.

## XV.—One is your Father.

THIS section of this collection is devoted to hymns which help, not in the ordinary way. They, indeed, seldom appear in hymn-books—the more's the pity. But they help many who find too much to dissent from in ordinary hymns to find any help therein.

### 127—THE UNIVERSAL PRAYER.

FATHER of All! in ev'ry Age,
　In ev'ry Clime ador'd,
By Saint, by Savage, and by Sage,
　Jehovah, Jove, or Lord!

Thou Great First Cause, least understood,
　Who all my Sense confin'd
To know but this, that Thou art Good,
　And that myself am blind:

Yet gave me, in this dark Estate,
　To see the Good from Ill;
And binding Nature fast in Fate,
　Left free the Human Will.

What Conscience dictates to be done,
　Or warns me not to do,
This, teach me more than Hell to shun,
　That, more than Heav'n pursue.

What Blessings thy free Bounty gives,
　Let me not cast away;
For God is pay'd when Man receives;
　T' enjoy is to obey.

Yet not to Earth's contracted Span
  Thy Goodness let me bound,
Or think Thee Lord alone of Man,
  When thousand Worlds are round.

Let not this weak, unknowing hand
  Presume thy bolts to throw,
And deal damnation round the land,
  On each I judge thy Foe.

If I am right, thy grace impart,
  Still in the right to stay;
If I am wrong, oh, teach my heart
  To find that better way.

Save me alike from foolish Pride,
  Or impious Discontent,
At aught thy Wisdom has deny'd
  Or aught thy Goodness lent.

Teach me to feel another's Woe,
  To hide the Fault I see;
That Mercy I to others show,
  That Mercy show to me.

Mean tho' I am, not wholly so,
  Since quick'ned by thy Breath;
Oh lead me wheresoe'er I go,
  Thro' this day's Life or Death.

This day, be Bread and Peace my Lot:
  All else beneath the Sun,
Thou know'st if best bestow'd or not;
  And let Thy Will be done.

To thee, whose Temple is all Space,
  Whose Altar Earth, Sea, Skies,
One Chorus let all Being raise,
  All Nature's Incense rise!

TUNE — "ABRIDGE."

Pope, the author of this hymn, was a Roman Catholic by creed. But in the above hymn he is catholic indeed.

A correspondent wrote me on behalf of some young Japanese friends, asking especially for the insertion of this hymn in the hope that "the time may come when even Christians, especially insular Protestant Christians, will arise to the full conception of the Holy One (Blessed be He!), that He has made of one Blood and of many honest beliefs all nations of the earth. In centuries hence, if the progress we hope for will be realised, surely hymns will be found or written in which all nations can join."

A correspondent in Italy writes of this hymn: "My grandfather made me learn it when I was five years old, and since then it has stuck to my memory as almost a kind of active faith, when things in the world in general seem wrong, and faith is very feeble. At such times there is wonderful rest in the poem, something quite above our usual petty ideas."

## 128—IMMORTAL LOVE, FOR EVER FULL.

WHITTIER, the Quaker poet, wrote poems which have passed into general use as hymns, even among the Friends, who are not much given to hymn-singing.

> IMMORTAL Love, for ever full,
>   For ever flowing free,
> For ever shared, for ever whole,
>   A never-ebbing sea!
>
> Our outward lips confess the Name
>   All other names above;
> Love only knoweth whence it came
>   And comprehendeth love.
>
> We may not climb the heavenly steeps
>   To bring the Lord Christ down;

In vain we search the lowest deeps,
  For him no depths can drown.

But warm, sweet, tender, even yet
  A present help is he:
And faith has still its Olivet,
  And love its Galilee.

The healing of his seamless dress
  Is by our beds of pain;
We touch him in life's throng and press,
  And we are whole again.

Through him the first fond prayers are said
  Our lips of childhood frame,
The last low whispers of our dead
  Are burdened with his name.

O Lord and Master of us all!
  Whate'er our name or sign,
We own thy sway, we hear thy call,
  We test our lives by thine.

                    TUNE — "ALBANO."

## 129 — OUR FRIEND, OUR BROTHER, AND OUR LORD.

OUR Friend, our Brother, and our Lord,
  What may thy service be?
Nor name, nor form, nor ritual word,
  But simply following thee.

Thy litanies, sweet offices
  Of love and gratitude;
Thy sacramental liturgies
  The joy of doing good.

The heart must ring thy Christmas bells,
 Thy inward altars raise;
Its faith and hopes thy canticles,
 And its obedience praise!

To thee our full humanity,
 Its joys and pains belong;
The wrong of man to man on thee
 Inflicts a deeper wrong.

We faintly hear, we dimly see,
 In differing phrase we pray;
But, dim or clear, we own thee
 The Light, the Truth, the Way!

Apart from thee all gain is loss,
 All labour vainly done;
The solemn shadow of thy cross
 Is better than the sun.

Alone, O Love ineffable!
 Thy saving name is given;
To turn aside from thee is hell,
 To walk with thee is heaven.

TUNE — "ST. HUGH."

In reply to an enquiry as to what hymns had helped her and her fellow-workers in the struggle which they carried on for a quarter of a century against the criminal system of state-patronised vice, Mrs. Josephine Butler replied: "Strange to say, I find it very difficult to select any special hymn which helped me in my soul or in my work. Psalms have been above all else 'Songs in the house of my pilgrimage,' but Whittier's 'Our Master' was most helpful to me in connection with the wide circle of persons of different countries, creeds, and characters with whom I have been sent to work — dear souls — to whom I am united in the common aim of seeking after righteousness, but some of whom seemed of the narrowly orthodox, to be very unsatisfactory on the religious side. God has given me a wider outlook, and a far greater charity based on an increasing admiration of all good. This hymn of Whittier will explain what I mean, and show you where my tempest-tossed bark has found a haven in calm waters."

## 130—LORD OF ALL BEING, THRONED AFAR.

OLIVER WENDELL HOLMES, the Autocrat of the Breakfast Table, was a Unitarian. He published this as a Sunday hymn on the last page of the " Professor of the Breakfast Table." It was speedily exploited as a hymn by the Methodists.

LORD of all being, throned afar,
Thy glory flames from sun and star;
Centre and soul of every sphere,
Yet to each loving heart how near.

Sun of our life, thy quickening ray
Sheds on our path the glow of day;
Star of our hope, thy softened light
Cheers the long watches of the night.

Our midnight is thy smile withdrawn;
Our noontide is thy gracious dawn;
Our rainbow arch, thy mercy's sign;
All, save the clouds of sin, are thine.

Lord of all life, below, above,
Whose light is truth, whose warmth is love,
Before thy ever-blazing throne
We ask no lustre of our own.

Grant us thy truth to make us free,
And kindly hearts that burn for thee,
Till all thy living altars claim
One holy light, one heavenly flame.

TUNE — " MARYTON."

## 131—SOULS OF MEN! WHY WILL YE SCATTER.

THIS contribution to the universal catholic section of my collection is from Faber, the Roman Catholic. It expresses a breadth of Christian charity not often found in men of his communion.

SOULS of men! why will ye scatter
    Like a crowd of frightened sheep?
Foolish hearts! why will ye wander
    From a love so true and deep?

Was there ever kinder shepherd
    Half so gentle, half so sweet,
As the Saviour Who would have us
    Come and gather round His feet?

There's a wideness in God's mercy,
    Like the wideness of the sea;
There's a kindness in His justice,
    Which is more than liberty.

There is no place where earth's sorrows
    Are more felt than up in Heaven;
There is no place where earth's failings
    Have such kindly judgment given.

There is plentiful redemption
    In the Blood that has been shed;
There is joy for all the members
    In the sorrows of the Head.

For the love of God is broader
    Than the measures of man's mind;
And the Heart of the Eternal
    Is most wonderfully kind.

Pining souls! come nearer Jesus,
  And oh! come not doubting thus,
But with faith that trusts more bravely
  His huge tenderness for us.

If our love were but more simple,
  We should take Him at his word;
And our lives would be all sunshine
  In the sweetness of our Lord.   Amen.

TUNE — "CLARION."

## 132 — WHAT I LIVE FOR.

THIS poem, by the late Mr. G. Linnæus Banks, has been sent me by Mr. Mayer, of the Children's Home, Bolton, as one which is morally and spiritually helpful to the people.

I LIVE for those who love me,
  Whose hearts are kind and true,
For the heaven that smiles above me,
  And awaits my spirit too;
For all human ties that bind me,
For the task by God assigned me,
For the bright hopes yet to find me,
  And the good that I can do.

I live to learn their story
  Who suffered for my sake;
To emulate their glory,
  And follow in their wake —
Bards, patriots, martyrs, sages,
The heroic of all ages,
Whose deeds crowd history's pages,
  And Time's great volume make.

I live to hold communion
  With all that is divine,

To feel there is a union
  'Twixt Nature's heart and mine;
To profit by affliction,
Reap truth from fields of fiction,
Grow wiser from conviction,
  And fulfil God's grand design.

I live to hail that season,
  By gifted ones foretold,
When men shall live by reason,
  And not alone by gold;
When man to man united,
And every wrong thing righted,
The whole world shall be lighted
  As Eden was of old.

I live for those who love me,
  For those who know me true,
For the heaven that smiles above me,
  And awaits my spirit too;
For the cause that lacks assistance,
For the wrong that needs resistance,
For the future in the distance,
  And the good that I can do.

## 133 — THE SPACIOUS FIRMAMENT ON HIGH.

ADDISON'S paraphrase of the Nineteenth Psalm is a brief and popular compendium of natural theology. The psalm was one of the favourites of St. Augustine.

THE spacious firmament on high,
  With all the blue ethereal sky,
And spangled heavens, — a shining frame, —
Their great Original proclaim.

The unwearied sun, from day to day,
Doth his Creator's power display,
And publishes to every land
The work of an Almighty hand.

Soon as the evening shades prevail,
The moon takes up the wondrous tale,
And, nightly, to the listening earth,
Repeats the story of her birth :
Whilst all the stars that round her burn,
And all the planets in their turn,
Confirm the tidings as they roll,
And spread the truth from pole to pole.

What though, in solemn silence all
Move round this dark terrestrial ball;
What though no real voice nor sound
Amidst their radiant orbs be found ;
In reason's ear they all rejoice,
And utter forth a glorious voice;
For ever singing as they shine —
The hand that made us is Divine.

TUNE — "FULDA."

"When only a youngster at school," writes a correspondent in the Isle of Man, "Addison's hymn had more attraction for me than a story in the 'Arabian Nights.'" This is, perhaps, putting it rather strongly; but, when a boy myself, I remember well committing it to memory, and the pleasure which it afforded me, — pleasure which, curiously enough, is linked by association with the effect produced by the first time I read a translation of Hesiod.

Another correspondent says that "at eight this hymn first taught me what poetry meant."

## XVI.—And All Ye are Brethren.

### 134—A JEWISH HYMN THAT HELPED.

THIS collection of Hymns that have Helped would be incomplete without, at least, one specimen of a Jewish hymn, and one or two which have helped thousands in the Roman Communion. I asked Mr. M. H. Spielmann, editor of the *Magazine of Art*, to help me to the most helpful Jewish hymn. He replied as follows:—

"Jews have no 'hymns,' properly so-called, though they have many poems of a hymnal sort, taking chiefly the form of praise. For myself, I may say that the 'Adown Olam' was to me the most helpful as a child and youth, and was the *point de départ*, and the base of all my subsequent reading, theological or philosophical. It is not merely a profession of faith, it is the complete exposition of the Jewish religion, and the supremest expression of comfort and consolation, so far as I am aware, in all our book of prayer."

The Rev. F. L. Cohen, joint editor of the *Book of Synagogue Music*, has kindly sent me a translation of the "Adôn 'Olam," the text of which is as follows:—

### ADÔN 'OLAM.

THE Universal Master reigned
 Ere yet created things took shape;
His might proclaimed Him King of all
When He to all existence gave;

And after all shall pass away,
'T is He alone shall grandly reign,
Who was, and is, and still shall be:
His glories all our worship have.

For He is One, no other power
Compares with Him, with Him consorts;

Without beginning, free from end,
Above what splendour men may crave.

[Without corporeality,
From change and variation free,
As unconjoined as undetached,
Alone in matchless power to save.]

He is my God, my Saviour lives,
My Rock in travail's time of woe;
My Banner and my Refuge He,
My Draught of Life when help I crave.

Into His hand my soul I trust,
Both when I sleep and when I wake;
And with my soul my body too:
God is with me, no fears enslave.

F. L. C.

N.B. — The verse in brackets above is usually omitted.

Speaking of this, Mr. Cohen says: "It is almost a literal translation, and reproduces the rhythm and the rhyme of the original Hebrew.

"We have a number of Table-Hymns (*Zemiroth*) chanted on the Sabbath before Grace. Of these, Psalm cxxvi. (we sing the Psalms in Hebrew, of course) and No. 10 'Sabbath Rest' in the publication of mine I enclose (p. 25) have proved very precious helps to many of us. Much help, too, has been derived from the hymn *Ma'ôz Tsur*, for *Hanucah* (the anniversary of the Maccabean Dedication), a copy of my English version of which (again closely reproducing the rhythm and rhyme of the Hebrew) I give on the back of 'Adôn 'Olam.'"

## 135.—AVE MARIA.

As many Protestants have never read the prayer which is said and sung all over Roman Christendom, I quote it here together with one of the best-known hymns to the Virgin:—

HAIL, Mary, full of grace; the Lord is with Thee: blessed art Thou among women, and blessed is the fruit of Thy womb, Jesus. Holy Mary, Mother of God, pray for us sinners, now and at the hour of our death. Amen.

AVE, Maria, gratia plena; Dominus tecum; benedicta tu in mulieribus, et benedictus fructus ventris tui, Jesus. Sancta Maria, Mater Dei, ora pro nobis peccatoribus, nunc et in hora mortis nostræ. Amen.

### 136.—AVE MARIS STELLA.

THIS is probably the oldest,—it dates from the ninth century,—best-known, most-used, and therefore, most helpful of all the hymns to the Mother of Jesus, which edify the Roman, and scandalise the Protestant, who forgets that if the spirit of the prayer or hymn be instinct with love, there are resources in the Chancery of Heaven for re-addressing petitions that may have been wrongly directed by mistake.

HAIL, bright Star of ocean,
   God's own Mother blest,
Ever-sinless Virgin,
   Gate of heavenly rest;

Taking that sweet Ave
   Which from Gabriel came,
Peace confirm within us,
   Changing Eva's name.

Break the captive's fetters;
   Light on blindness pour;
All our ills expelling,
   Every bliss implore.

Show thyself a mother;
 May the Word Divine,
Born for us thine Infant,
 Hear our prayers through thine.

Virgin all excelling,
 Mildest of the mild,
Freed from guilt, preserve us
 Meek and undefiled;

Keep our life all spotless,
 Make our way secure,
Till we find in Jesus
 Joy for evermore.

Through the highest Heaven
 To the Almighty Three,
Father, Son, and Spirit,
 One same glory be.

AVE maris stella,
 Dei Mater alma,
Atque semper virgo,
Felix cœli porta.

Sumens illud Ave,
Gabrielis ore,
Funda nos in pace,
Mutans Hevæ nomen.

Solve vincla reis,
Profer lumen cæcis,
Mala nostra pelle,
Bona cuncta posce.

Monstra te esse matrem
Sumat per te preces,
Qui pro nobis natus,
Tulit esse tuus.

Virgo singularis,
Inter omnes mitis,
Nos culpis solutos,
Mites fac et castos.

Vitam præsta puram
Iter para tutum,
Ut videntes Jesum,
Semper collætemur.

Sit laus Deo Patri
Summo Christo decus,
Spiritui Sancto,
Tribus honor unus.

## 137—FAITH OF OUR FATHERS.

The following Roman Catholic hymn is a kind of defiant war-song, the note of which endears it much to the faithful.

(The words in Italics apply to Ireland, and may be substituted for the text below when fitting.)

FAITH of our Fathers! living still,
   In spite of dungeon, fire, and sword:
Oh, { *Ireland's* / how our } hearts beat high with joy
Whene'er { *they* / we } hear that glorious word:
Faith of our Fathers! Holy Faith!
We will be true to thee till death.

Our Fathers, chained in prisons dark,
Were still in heart and conscience free;
How sweet would be their children's fate,
If they, like them, could die for thee!
      Faith of our Fathers, etc.

Faith of our Fathers! Mary's prayers
{ *Shall keep our country fast to thee;* }
{ Shall win our country back to thee; }
And through the truth that comes from God,
{ *Oh, we shall prosper and be free.* }
{ England shall then indeed be free. }
  Faith of our Fathers, etc.

Faith of our Fathers! we will love
Both friend and foe in all our strife:
And preach thee too, as love knows how,
By kindly words and virtuous life.
  Faith of our Fathers, etc.

       TUNE — "SWISS AIR."

This hymn, with the change of a word or two in the third verse, is used by the American Unitarians as a metrical embodiment of their history and aspirations.

## 138 — ETERNAL FATHER, STRONG TO SAVE.

THIS is one of Sir Evelyn Wood's favourites. It was written by the late William Whiting, choirmaster of Winchester College, and is much used at sea; and, when the wind blows hard, by those on land.

ETERNAL Father, strong to save,
 Whose arm hath bound the restless wave,
Who bidd'st the mighty ocean deep
Its own appointed limits keep:
  Oh, hear us when we cry to Thee
  For those in peril on the sea.

O Christ, Whose voice the waters heard
And hush'd their raging at Thy word,
Who walkedst on the foaming deep,
And calm amid the storm didst sleep;

Oh, hear us when we cry to Thee
For those in peril on the sea.

O Holy Spirit, Who didst brood
Upon the waters dark and rude,
And bid their angry tumult cease,
And give, for wild confusion, peace ;
    Oh, hear us when we cry to Thee
    For those in peril on the sea.

O Trinity of love and power,
Our brethren shield in danger's hour;
From rock and tempest, fire and foe,
Protect them wheresoe'er they go;
    Thus evermore shall rise to Thee
    Glad hymns of praise from land and sea. Amen.
                     Tune—" Melita."

## 139.—THE LORD'S SUPPER.

George Rawson wrote this Communion hymn for the Baptists in 1857. It has been appropriated extensively by other denominations, whose use of it is the best testimony to its helpfulness.

BY Christ redeemed, in Christ restored,
    We keep the memory adored
And show the death of our dear Lord,
        Until He come.

His body broken in our stead
Is here, in this memorial bread,
And so our feeble love is fed,
        Until He come.

The drops of His dread agony,
His life-blood shed for us, we see;
The wine shall tell the mystery,
        Until He come.

And thus that dark betrayal night
With the last advent we unite,
By one blest chain of loving rite,
        Until He come.

Until the trump of God be heard,
Until the ancient graves be stirred,
And with the great commanding word
        The Lord shall come.

O blessed hope! with this elate,
Let not our hearts be desolate,
But, strong in faith, in patience wait,
        Until He come.
        TUNE — "SOMERCOTES."

## 140 — A FEW MORE YEARS SHALL ROLL.

A HYMN of Dr. Bonar's, written in 1842, forty years before his death.

A FEW more years shall roll,
  A few more seasons come,
And we shall be with those that rest,
  Asleep within the tomb;
  Then, O my Lord, prepare
  My soul for that great day;
Oh, wash me in Thy precious Blood,
  And take my sins away.

  A few more suns shall set
  O'er these dark hills of time,
And we shall be where suns are not,
  A far serener clime:
  Then, O my Lord, prepare
  My soul for that bright day;
Oh, wash me in Thy precious Blood,
  And take my sins away.

A few more storms shall beat
On this wild rocky shore,
And we shall be where tempests cease,
And surges swell no more:
Then, O my Lord, prepare
My soul for that calm day;
Oh, wash me in Thy precious Blood,
And take my sins away.

A few more struggles here,
A few more partings o'er,
A few more toils, a few more tears,
And we shall weep no more:
Then, O my Lord, prepare
My soul for that blest day;
Oh, wash me in Thy precious Blood,
And take my sins away.

'T is but a little while
And He shall come again,
Who died that we might live, Who lives
That we with Him may reign:
Then, O my Lord, prepare
My soul for that glad day;
Oh, wash me in Thy precious Blood,
And take my sins away.   Amen.

TUNE—"LEOMINSTER" OR "CHALVEY."

## 141—WE PLOUGH THE FIELDS AND SCATTER.

CLAUDIUS's "Wir pflügen und wir streuen" was first published in German in 1782. It is used both in Germany and in England as a harvest hymn. I give Miss T. M. Campbell's English version.

WE plough the fields and scatter
The good seed on the land,

But it is fed and water'd
  By God's Almighty Hand;
He sends the snow in winter,
  The warmth to swell the grain,
The breezes and the sunshine,
  And soft refreshing rain.
    All good gifts around us
      Are sent from Heav'n above,
    Then thank the Lord, Oh, thank the Lord,
      For all His love.

He only is the Maker
  Of all things near and far;
He paints the wayside flower,
  He lights the evening star;
The winds and waves obey Him,
  By Him the birds are fed;
Much more to us, His children,
  He gives our daily bread.
    All good gifts around us
      Are sent from Heav'n above,
    Then thank the Lord, Oh, thank the Lord,
      For all His love.

We thank Thee then, O Father,
  For all things bright and good,
The seed-time and the harvest,
  Our life, our health, our food;
Accept the gifts we offer
  For all Thy love imparts,
And, what Thou most desirest,
  Our humble, thankful hearts.
    All good gifts around us
      Are sent from Heav'n above,
    Then thank the Lord, Oh, thank the Lord,
      For all His love.   Amen.

TUNE — THE WELL-KNOWN ONE BY J. A. P. SCHULZ.

## XVII.—Death.

### 142—COME, LET US JOIN OUR FRIENDS ABOVE.

THE Bishop of Hereford writes me that he thinks the fourth verse "one of the finest in the whole range of hymnology." It is the favourite Wesleyan funeral hymn. The author of "Methodist Hymn-Book Notes" used several pages in describing the affecting and happy incidents in connection with the use of this hymn, and says he suppresses many other pages for want of space.

COME, let us join our friends above
 Who have obtained the prize,
And, on the eagle-wings of love,
 To joys celestial rise.

Let all the saints terrestrial sing,
 With those to glory gone;
For all the servants of our King,
 On earth and heaven, are one.

One family we dwell in Him,—
 One church, above, beneath;
Though now divided by the stream,
 The narrow stream of death.

One army of the living God,
 To His command we bow;
Part of His host have crossed the flood,
 And part are crossing now.

Ten thousand to their endless home
 This solemn moment fly:
And we are to the margin come,
 And we expect to die.

E'en now by faith we join our hands
  With those that went before:
And greet the blood-besprinkled bands
  On the eternal shore.

Our spirits too shall quickly join,
  Like theirs with glory crowned,
And shout to see our Captain's sign,
  To hear His trumpet sound.

Be Thou, O God, our constant guide,
  And when the word is given,
Then, Lord of Hosts, the waves divide,
  And land us all in heaven.

                    TUNE — "GRETTON."

## 143 — GIVE ME THE WINGS OF FAITH TO RISE.

THIS favourite hymn of Watts was published in 1709, and it has been in general use among all sections of the Church for a century.

GIVE me the wings of faith to rise
  Within the veil, and see
The saints above, how great their joys!
  How bright their glories be!

Once they were mourning here below
  And wet their couch with tears;
They wrestled hard, as we do now,
  With sins and doubts and fears.

I ask them whence their victory came?
  They, with united breath,
Ascribe their conquest to the Lamb,
  Their triumph to His death.

They marked the footsteps that He trod,
  His zeal inspired their breast;
And, following their Incarnate God,
  Possess the promised rest.

Our glorious Leader claims our praise
  For His own pattern given,
While the long cloud of witnesses
  Shows the same path to heaven.

TUNE—"MYLON."

## 144—HEAR WHAT THE VOICE OF HEAVEN PROCLAIMS.

THIS hymn, also by Watts, is much used at burials.

HEAR what the voice from heaven proclaims
  For all the pious dead:
Sweet is the savour of their names,
  And soft their sleeping bed.

They die in Jesus and are blest;
  How kind their slumbers are!
From sufferings and from sins released
  And freed from every snare.

Far from this world of toil and strife,
  They're present with the Lord;
The labours of their mortal life
  End in a large reward.

TUNE—"BEATITUDO."

## 145—HOW BLEST THE RIGHTEOUS WHEN HE DIES.

THIS hymn by Mrs. Barbauld is quoted by Thomas Carlyle when describing the death of Oliver Cromwell.

How blest the righteous when he dies!
   When sinks a weary soul to rest,
How mildly beam the closing eyes,
How gently heaves the expiring breast!

So fades a summer cloud away:
So sinks the gale when storms are o'er:
So gently shuts the eye of day;
So dies a wave along the shore.

A holy quiet reigns around,
A calm which life nor death destroys:
Nothing disturbs that peace profound,
Which his unfettered soul enjoys.

Farewell, conflicting hopes and fears,
Where lights and shades alternate dwell!
How bright the unchanging morn appears!
Farewell, inconstant world, farewell!

Life's labour done, as sinks the clay,
Light from its load the spirit flies;
While heaven and earth combine to say,
How blest the righteous when he dies!

TUNE — "CUYLER."

Mrs. Barbauld is perhaps even better known by her lines on Life, written when she was over seventy: —

"Life! we've been long together,
   Through pleasant and through cloudy weather.
'T is hard to part when friends are dear —
Perhaps 't will cost a sigh, a tear; —
   Then steal away; give little warning,
Choose thine own time;
Say not Good-night, — but in some brighter clime,
   Bid me Good-morning!"

## 146 — SLEEP ON, BELOVED.

This funeral hymn, which has attained even greater vogue in America than in this country, is by Miss Sarah Doudney. It was the hymn sung at Mr. Spurgeon's funeral.

SLEEP on, belovèd, sleep, and take thy rest;
   Lay down thy head upon thy Saviour's breast:
We love thee well; but Jesus loves thee best —
   Good-night! Good-night! Good-night!

Calm is thy slumber as an infant's sleep;
But thou shalt wake no more to toil and weep:
Thine is a perfect rest, secure and deep —
                    Good-night!

Until the shadows from this earth are cast;
Until He gathers in His sheaves at last;
Until the twilight gloom is overpast —
                    Good-night!

Until the Easter glory lights the skies;
Until the dead in Jesus shall arise,
And He shall come, but not in lowly guise —
                    Good-night!

Until made beautiful by Love Divine,
Thou, in the likeness of Thy Lord shalt shine,
And He shall bring that golden crown of thine —
                    Good-night!

Only "good-night," belovèd — not "farewell!"
A little while, and all His saints shall dwell
In hallowed union, indivisible —
                    Good-night!

Until we meet again before His throne,
Clothed in the spotless robe He gives His own,
Until we know even as we are known —
>> Good-night!

TUNE — MR. SANKEY'S.

## 147 — NOW THE LABOURER'S TASK IS O'ER.

THIS hymn is one of the favourites of Her Majesty the Queen, and is frequently selected by her to be sung at the funerals of members of her family. It was written by the Rev. J. Ellerton, and first published by the Society for Promoting Christian Knowledge, in "Church Hymns," 1871.

NOW the labourer's task is o'er,
   Now the battle day is past;
Now upon the farther shore
   Lands the voyager at last.
FATHER, in Thy gracious keeping
Leave we now Thy servant sleeping.

There the tears of earth are dried;
   There its hidden things are clear;
There the work of life is tried
   By a juster Judge than here.
FATHER, in Thy gracious keeping
Leave we now Thy servant sleeping.

There the sinful souls, that turn
   To the Cross their dying eyes,
All the love of CHRIST shall learn
   At His Feet in Paradise.
FATHER, in Thy gracious keeping
Leave we now Thy servant sleeping.

There no more the powers of hell
   Can prevail to mar their peace;
CHRIST the LORD shall guard them well,
   He who died for their release.
FATHER, in Thy gracious keeping
Leave we now Thy servant sleeping.

"Earth to earth, and dust to dust,"
   Calmly now the words we say,
Left behind we wait in trust
   For the Resurrection-day.
FATHER, in Thy gracious keeping
Leave we now Thy servant sleeping.
                     AMEN.
            TUNE — "REQUIESCAT."

## 148 — I LAY ME DOWN TO SLEEP.

FOUND UNDER THE PILLOW OF A SOLDIER, WHO DIED IN A HOSPITAL IN SOUTH CAROLINA DURING THE AMERICAN WAR.

I LAY me down to sleep,
   With little thought or care,
Whether my waking find
   Me here or there.

A bowing, burdened head,
   That only asks to rest
Unquestioning upon
   A loving breast.

My good right hand forgets
   Its cunning now,
To march the weary march
   I know not how.

I am not eager, bold,
   Nor strong — all that is past:

I am ready not to do,
   At last, at last.

My half-day's work is done,
   And this is all my part;
I give a patient God
   My patient heart.

And grasp His banner still
   Though all its blue be dim,
These stripes no less than stars
   Lead after Him.

## XVIII.—Heaven.

### 149—JERUSALEM, MY HAPPY HOME.

THE famous song made by F. B. P. at the end of the sixteenth century begins:—

   Hierusalem, my happy home;
     When shall I come to thee:
   When shall my sorrowes have an end,
     Thy ioys when shall I see.

There are twenty-six verses, some of them very quaint. The most popular modern version "given in the text" is believed to be by Montgomery.

JERUSALEM, my happy home;
   Name ever dear to me :
When shall my labours have an end
   In joy and peace and thee!

When shall these eyes thy heaven-built walls
   And pearly gates behold,
Thy bulwarks with salvation strong,
   And streets of shining gold?

There happier bowers than Eden's bloom,
  Nor sin, nor sorrow know;
Blest seats, through rude and stormy scenes,
  I onward press to you.

Why should I shrink from pain and woe,
  Or feel at death dismay?
I've Canaan's goodly land in view,
  And realms of endless day.

Apostles, martyrs, prophets there,
  Around my Saviour stand;
And soon my friends in Christ below
  Will join the glorious band.

Jerusalem, my happy home,
  My soul still pants for thee:
Then shall my labours have an end,
  When I thy joys shall see.

TUNE — "SOUTHWELL" OR "BEULAH."

## 150 — THERE IS A LAND OF PURE DELIGHT.

WHETHER Watts wrote this at Southampton, inspired by a view of the Isle of Wight or of the New Forest, is uncertain. But whatever the scene that suggested these familiar stanzas, they have helped myriads to cross with steadier nerve the swelling flood, on the brink of which we shivering stand and fear to launch away.

THERE is a land of pure delight,
  Where saints immortal reign;
Infinite day excludes the night,
  And pleasures banish pain.

There everlasting spring abides
  And never-withering flowers;
Death, like a narrow sea, divides
  This heavenly land from ours.

Sweet fields beyond the swelling flood
  Stand dressed in living green;
So to the Jews old Canaan stood,
  While Jordan rolled between.

But timorous mortals start and shrink
  To cross this narrow sea,
And linger, shivering on the brink,
  And fear to launch away.

Oh, could we make our doubts remove,
  Those gloomy doubts that rise:
And see the Canaan that we love
  With unbeclouded eyes:

Could we but climb where Moses stood,
  And view the landscape o'er,
Not Jordan's stream, nor death's cold flood,
  Should fright us from the shore.

                    TUNE — " BEULAH."

## BERNARD OF CLUNY'S "SWEET AND BLESSED COUNTRY."

OUT of three thousand lines of a satire written by Bernard, a monk of Cluny, in the twelfth century, Dr. Neale has extracted three hymns, which, in his free translation, have become extremely popular. It is significant of the difference between the centuries that the twelfth-century satirist is overwhelmed by the awe of heaven and the horror of hell, whereas his nineteenth-century adapter sings exultantly of heaven alone.

## 151—BRIEF LIFE IS HERE OUR PORTION.

BRIEF life is here our portion,
  Brief sorrow, short-lived care:
The life that knows no ending,
  The tearless life, is *there*.

O happy retribution!
  Short toil, eternal rest;
For mortals and for sinners
  A mansion with the blest!

There grief is turned to pleasure,
  Such pleasure, as below
No human voice can utter,
  No human heart can know.
And now we fight the battle,
  But then shall wear the crown
Of full and everlasting
  And passionless renown.

And now we watch and struggle,
  And now we live in hope,
And Sion, in her anguish,
  With Babylon must cope.
But He whom now we trust in
  Shall then be seen and known,
And they that know and see Him
  Shall have Him for their own.

The morning shall awaken,
  The shadows shall decay,
And each true-hearted servant
  Shall shine as doth the day:
Yes; God, our King and Portion,
  In fulness of His grace,
We then shall see for ever,
  And worship face to face.

*O sweet and blessèd country,*
  *The home of God's elect!*
*O sweet and blessèd country*
  *That eager hearts expect!*

*Jesus, in mercy bring us*
  *To that dear land of rest;*
*Who art, with God the Father,*
  *And Spirit, ever blest.*

              TUNE — "ST. ALPHEGE."

## 152 — FOR THEE, O DEAR, DEAR COUNTRY.

FOR thee, O dear, dear country!
  Mine eyes their vigils keep;
For very love beholding
  Thy happy name, they weep:
The mention of thy glory
  Is unction to the breast,
And medicine in sickness,
  And love, and life, and rest.

O one, O only mansion!
  O Paradise of joy!
Where tears are ever banished,
  And smiles have no alloy.
With jaspers glow thy bulwarks,
  Thy streets with emeralds blaze;
The sardius and the topaz
  Unite in thee their rays.

Thine ageless walls are bonded
  With amethyst unpriced;
The saints build up its fabric,
  And the corner-stone is Christ.
The cross is all thy splendour,
  The Crucified thy praise;
His laud and benediction
  Thy ransomed people raise.

Thou hast no shore, fair ocean!
  Thou hast no time, bright day!
Dear fountain of refreshment,
  To pilgrims far away!
Upon the Rock of Ages
  They raise thy holy tower;
Thine is the victor's laurel,
  And thine the golden dower.

*O sweet and blessèd country,*
  *The home of God's elect!*
*O sweet and blessèd country,*
  *That eager hearts expect!*
*Jesus, in mercy bring us*
  *To that dear land of rest;*
*Who art, with God the Father,*
  *And Spirit, ever blest.*

TUNE—"JENNER."

## 153—JERUSALEM THE GOLDEN.

JERUSALEM the golden,
  With milk and honey blest,
Beneath thy contemplation
  Sink heart and voice opprest.
I know not, Oh, I know not,
  What joys await us there;
What radiancy of glory,
  What light beyond compare!

They stand, those halls of Sion,
  All jubilant with song,
And bright with many an angel,
  And all the martyr throng.
The Prince is ever in them;
  The daylight is serene;
The pastures of the blessèd
  Are decked in glorious sheen.

HYMNS THAT HAVE HELPED. 257

> There is the throne of David;
>   And there, from care released,
> The shout of them that triumph,
>   The song of them that feast;
> And they who, with their Leader,
>   Have conquered in the fight,
> For ever and for ever
>   Are clad in robes of white.
>
> *O sweet and blessèd country,*
>   *The home of God's elect!*
> *O sweet and blessèd country,*
>   *That eager hearts expect!*
> *Jesus, in mercy bring us*
>   *To that dear land of rest;*
> *Who art, with God the Father,*
>   *And Spirit, ever blest.*
>                 TUNE—"EWING."

## 154—NEAR US STANDING HERE FORGETFUL.

WHEN the miners were imprisoned in Pontypridd mine, expecting never again to see the light of day, they sang the following verse of a hymn well known in Wales:

> IN the waves and mighty waters
>   No one will support my head,
> But my Saviour, my Beloved,
>   Who was stricken in my stead:
> In the flood of death's dark river
>   He will hold my head above;
> I shall through the waves go singing
>   For one look of Him I love.

> YN y dyfroedd mawr a'r tonau
>   Nid oes neb a ddeil fy mhen

Ond fy anwyl Briod Iesu
  A fu farw ar y pren
Cyfaill yw yn afon angeu
  Ddeil fy mhen yn uwch na'r don
Golwg arno wna i mi ganu
  Yn yr afon ddofn hon.

I asked Mr. Burt if he could tell me what hymns had been sung by North-country miners in similar circumstances, but he did not know.

# APPENDICES.

## APPENDIX I.

### SOME LETTERS FROM WORKING-MEN.

ONE of the difficulties which I have had to contend with has been the multitude of letters received from unknown correspondents, who have kindly responded to my appeal, and certify that this, that, or the other hymn marked an epoch in their life. It is quite impossible for me to quote from all, or even from many of those letters, neither can I by any possibility print all the hymns which have thus received the hall-mark of personal helpfulness, but one or two extracts may be made, chiefly from those upon whom the burden of life rests somewhat heavily.

Thomas Martin, a Darlington engineer, writing as one of the "Sons of Toil," says:—

"We, sir, have our helps as well as those above us. I can assure you that the sweet songs of the sanctuary of the soul have given us weary ones many a solace and a lift; and amidst the jarring and wrangling of the sectarians over their creeds and dogmas, how sweet is that inspired hymn No. 169 in Dr. Martineau's collection of 'Hymns of Praise and Prayer,' commencing thus—

> Spirit of Truth, be Thou my Guide,
> O clasp my hand in Thine.
> And let me never quit Thy side,
> Thy comforts are divine.
>
> Pride scorns Thee for Thy lowly mien;
> But who like Thee can rise
> Above this toilsome sordid scene,
> Beyond the holy skies.
>
> Weak is Thine eye, and soft Thy voice;
> But wondrous is Thy might
> To make the wretched soul rejoice,
> And give the simple light.

I can assure you, sir, that we have our consolations and help from such-like hymns; and many more."

Another working-man sends me a letter expressing his earnest hope that, whatever else is left out, I will take care to include No. 28 in Sankey's hymn-book; the hymn beginning, "I left it all with Jesus, long ago." Speaking of his own experience, he says he passed through a period of much tribulation, seeking peace and finding none:—

"I thought I had done my best, but still that was unsatisfactory. Something always seemed to be kept back; something that ought to have come out and did not, or rather, perhaps I should say that was not fully understood by the one to whom it was told. I had no doubt of my wish to repent, no doubt of my willingness to make every reparation in my power, but still peace would not come. At last I took it all straight to Jesus, and the burden rolled away from my heart. That is why I love No. 28 of Sankey's collection of Sacred Songs and Solos."

Hymns often act in this fashion. They cling to the memory, and by supplying the right word at the right time, act as the "open sesame" to the treasure which had been long and vainly sought.

An adult class at a friend's school at Darlington, being asked to say which hymns had helped them most, named, "I know not what awaits me," with the chorus, "Where He may lead, I'll follow" as the first favourite; the second, "When our heads are bowed with woe;" the third, "In the secret of His presence, hangs my soul's delight;" the fourth, "Oh, safe to the Rock that is higher than I."

A mechanic of Oldham tells how — when work was slack and hands were being dismissed, and no one knew whose turn it would be next — he was mightily sustained by a verse in Cowper's hymn, "Sometimes a light surprises." The verse which did him good, and seemed to him a message from God, was this, after the verse ending, "E'en let the unknown to-morrow bring with it what it may":—

> It can bring with it nothing,
>   But He will bear us through;
> Who gives the lilies clothing
>   Will clothe His people too.
> Beneath the spreading heavens,
>   No creature but is fed;
> And He who feeds the ravens
>   Will give His children bread.

Many a time that verse has cheered him and given him good heart to face the worst in the gloomiest of bad times.

# APPENDIX I. 261

I have said that from the uttermost parts of the earth I have received communications, and there are few places more out of the way than the Chatham Islands, although this year they have been favoured with a bi-monthly postal service. My correspondent, who uses the *nom de plume* " Tabitha," says that her husband well remembers when nine months elapsed before they heard from the outer world. Once a year a man-of-war anchors for a few days off the island, but the islanders, for the most part, live secluded from the outer world, weaving their own wool, supplying their own needs in primitive patriarchal fashion. My correspondent quotes, as the two verses which have helped her, the following: —

> And when I'm to die,
> " Receive me," I'll cry.
> For Jesus has loved me,
> I cannot tell why.
>
> But this do I find,
> That we two are joined,
> That He'll not be in glory,
> And leave me behind.

There are many hymns which have played no small part in the lives of men, which, however, I cannot include in this collection. Take, for instance, the hymn, " How bright these glorious spirits shine."

In the life of Duncan Matheson, Scottish Evangelist, we read that on the first Sabbath after he arrived at Balaclava, he and one or more of the 93rd Highlanders retired to a ravine, read, prayed, and sang the battle-song of David and Luther, " God is our refuge and our strength ;" and on page 70 to 71 we read : One night, weary and sad, returning from Sebastopol to the old stable at Balaclava where he lodged, his strength gone, sickened with the sights he had seen, depressed by the thought that the siege seemed no nearer an end, so, trudging along in mud knee-deep, he looked up and noticed the stars shining calmly in the clear sky ; instinctively his weary heart mounted heavenward, thinking of " the rest that remaineth for the people of God," he began to sing aloud, —

> How bright these glorious spirits shine.

Next day, though wet and stormy, he went out and came upon a soldier in rags, standing under an old verandah for shelter ; his naked toes were showing through worn-out boots. Matheson, speaking words of encouragement, gave him half-a-sovereign to purchase shoes. The soldier thanked him, and said : " I am not what I was yesterday. Last night, as I was thinking of our miserable condition, I grew tired of life, and said to myself . . . I can bear this no longer, and may as well put an end to it. So I took my musket and went down yonder in a desperate state, about eleven o'clock; but as I got round the point, I heard some person singing ' How bright these glorious spirits shine;' and I remembered the old tune and the Sabbath-school where we used to sing it. I felt ashamed of being so cowardly, and said: Here is someone as badly off as myself, and yet he is not giving in. I felt, too, he had something to make him happy which I had not, but I began to hope I too might get the same happiness. I returned to my tent, and to-day I am resolved to *seek the one thing*." "Do you know who the singer was?" asked the missionary. "No," was the reply. "Well," said the other, "It was I." Tears rushed into the soldier's eyes, and handing back the half-sovereign, he said: "Never, sir, can I take it from you after what you have been the means of doing for me."

## APPENDIX II.

### A LIST OF A BEST HUNDRED HYMNS.

EARLY in 1887 the Editors of *The Sunday at Home* invited their readers to send lists of the Hundred English Hymns which stood highest in their esteem. Nearly three thousand five hundred persons responded to the invitation; and by the majority of votes the following hundred were selected.

The first on the list, " Rock of Ages," received 3,215 votes; the last, "Sometimes a light surprises," 866. It was only to be expected that the former hymn would prove the most popular of all; but the three next to it each received about 3,000 votes, — " Abide with me," " Jesu, Lover of my soul," and " Just as I am."

| | HYMN. | AUTHOR. |
|---|---|---|
| 1. | Rock of Ages, cleft for me | *Toplady.* |
| 2. | Abide with me; fast falls the eventide | *Lyte.* |
| 3. | Jesu! Lover of my soul | *C. Wesley.* |
| 4. | Just as I am, without one plea | *C. Elliott.* |
| 5. | How sweet the name of Jesus sounds | *J. Newton.* |
| 6. | My God and Father, while I stray | *C. Elliott.* |
| 7. | Nearer, my God, to Thee | *Mrs. Adams.* |
| 8. | Sun of my soul, Thou Saviour dear | *Keble.* |
| 9. | I heard the voice of Jesus say | *H. Bonar.* |

| HYMN. | AUTHOR. |
|---|---|
| 10. Art thou weary, art thou languid? | *Stephen the Sabaite.* |
| 11. For ever with the Lord | *Jas. Montgomery.* |
| 12. God moves in a mysterious way | *Cowper.* |
| 13. From Greenland's icy mountains | *R. Heber.* |
| 14. When I survey the wondrous cross | *Watts.* |
| 15. Lead, kindly Light, amid the encircling gloom | *Newman.* |
| 16. Hark! the herald angels sing | *C. Wesley.* |
| 17. All praise to Thee, my God, this night | *T. Ken.* |
| 18. A few more years shall roll | *H. Bonar.* |
| 19. O God, our help in ages past | *Watts.* |
| 20. Our blest Redeemer, ere He breathed | *Harriet Auber.* |
| 21. All hail the power of Jesu's name | *E. Perronet.* |
| 22. Eternal Father! strong to save | *W. Whiting.* |
| 23. Holy, holy, holy! Lord God Almighty | *Heber.* |
| 24. Guide me, O Thou Great Jehovah | *W. Williams.* |
| 25. There is a fountain filled with blood | *Cowper.* |
| 26. Lo, He comes with clouds descending | *C. Wesley.* |
| 27. At even, ere the sun was set | *H. Twells.* |
| 28. Awake! my soul, and with the sun | *T. Ken.* |
| 29. Hark! my soul, it is the Lord | *Cowper.* |
| 30. All people that on earth do dwell | *W. Kethe.* |
| 31. Brief life is here our portion | *Bernard of Cluny.* |
| 32. Jesus shall reign where'er the sun | *Watts.* |
| 33. Jesus! the very thought of Thee | *Bernard of Clairvaux.* |
| 34. Hark! hark, my soul; angelic songs are swelling | *Faber.* |
| 35. Jerusalem, my happy home | *Anon.* |
| 36. Jerusalem the golden | *Bernard of Cluny.* |
| 37. Oft in danger, oft in woe | *H. K. White.* |
| 38. Come, let us join our cheerful songs | *Watts.* |
| 39. Thy way, not mine, O Lord | *H. Bonar.* |
| 40. Father, I know that all my life | *A. L. Waring.* |
| 41. Come, ye thankful people, come | *Alford.* |
| 42. Onward, Christian soldiers | *Baring-Gould.* |
| 43. I lay my sins on Jesus | *Bonar.* |
| 44. O for a closer walk with God | *Cowper.* |
| 45. O worship the King, all glorious above | *R. Grant.* |
| 46. Brightest and best of the sons of the morning | *R. Heber.* |
| 47. As pants the hart for cooling streams | *Tate and Brady.* |
| 48. Sweet Saviour! bless us ere we go | *Faber.* |
| 49. Hail to the Lord's Anointed | *Montgomery.* |
| 50. Pleasant are Thy courts above | *Lyte.* |
| 51. Great God! what do I see and hear? | *Ringwaldt.* |
| 52. There is a land of pure delight | *Watts.* |
| 53. O timely happy, timely wise | *J. Keble.* |
| 54. Christians, awake: salute the happy morn | *John Byrom.* |

| HYMN. | AUTHOR. |
|---|---|
| 55. Prayer is the soul's sincere delight | Jas. Montgomery. |
| 56. Saviour, again to Thy dear name we raise | J. Ellerton. |
| 57. The Church's one foundation | S. J. Stone. |
| 58. Soldiers of Christ, arise | C. Wesley. |
| 59. Weary of earth and laden with my sin | Rev. S. J. Stone. |
| 60. Christian, seek not yet repose | C. Elliott. |
| 61. O Day of rest and gladness | C. Wordsworth. |
| 62. Christ the Lord is risen to-day | C. Wesley. |
| 63. O Paradise! O Paradise | F. W. Faber. |
| 64. I need Thee, precious Jesus | F. Whitfield. |
| 65. Safe in the arms of Jesus | Mrs. Van Alstyne. |
| 66. O for a heart to praise my God | C. Wesley. |
| 67. Hark! the glad sound! the Saviour comes | Doddridge. |
| 68. Come unto Me, ye weary | W. C. Dix. |
| 69. My faith looks up to Thee | Ray Palmer. |
| 70. There is a green hill far away | Mrs. Alexander. |
| 71. Before Jehovah's awful throne | Watts. |
| 72. O Jesus, I have promised | J. E. Bode. |
| 73. The Son of God goes forth to war | R. Heber. |
| 74. Not all the blood of beasts | Watts. |
| 75. I was a wandering sheep | H. Bonar. |
| 76. O God of Bethel, by Whose hand | Doddridge. |
| 77. Peace, perfect peace | E. H. Bickersteth. |
| 78. O come, all ye faithful, joyful and triumphant | Anon. |
| 79. The King of Love my Shepherd is | H. W. Baker. |
| 80. Through all the changing scenes of life | Tate and Brady. |
| 81. Take my life, and let it be | F. R. Havergal. |
| 82. While shepherds watched their flocks by night | Tate. |
| 83. My God, and is Thy table spread | Doddridge. |
| 84. Jesus Christ is risen to-day | Anon. |
| 85. I could not do without Thee | F. R. Havergal. |
| 86. Jesus lives! no longer now | C. F. Gilbert. |
| 87. Come, Thou Fount of every blessing | R. Robinson. |
| 88. As with gladness men of old | W. C. Dix. |
| 89. O for a thousand tongues to sing | C. Wesley. |
| 90. Saviour! breathe an evening blessing | Jas. Edmeston. |
| 91. Sweet the moments, rich in blessing | Jas. Allen. |
| 92. Let us, with a gladsome mind | Milton. |
| 93. O happy band of pilgrims | Dr. J. M. Neale. |
| 94. Days and moments quickly flying | E. Caswall. |
| 95. Jesus calls us o'er the tumult | Mrs. Alexander. |
| 96. Glorious things of Thee are spoken | J. Newton. |
| 97. O Lord, how happy should we be | J. Anstice. |
| 98. Tell me the old, old story | Mrs. Hankey. |
| 99. Lord, I hear of showers of blessing | Eliz. Codner. |
| 100. Sometimes a light surprises | Cowper. |

These one hundred hymns were published by the Religious Tract Society in a threepenny pamphlet now out of print. The above list was sent out together with the appeal for information as to hymns that have helped. Hence in some cases, notably those of Mr. Massingham (of the *Daily Chronicle*), the Head Master of Marlborough College, and the Bishop of Hereford, the hymns quoted as those which helped them were, in addition to others, contained in the *Sunday at Home* list.

# APPENDIX III.

## HYMNS AND THOSE WHOM THEY HAVE HELPED.

THE following is a very rough and imperfect classification which I hope my readers will enable me to improve materially before the next edition. Some correspondents sent in so many hymns that had helped them that I could not quote them all. Canon Shuttleworth, for instance, mentioned a hundred, accompanying the list by the following characteristic note:

"I quite expect this list is very different from most. I hate with a holy hatred all sentimentalist maunderings, all feeble religiosities, all diseased raptures or sorrows. To help men, hymns should be manful."

I have been compelled in this, and in similar cases, to quote only five or six hymns, giving preference to those that are different from most. Mr. Gladstone's favourite hymns may be said to be almost universal favourites, whereas each one, as a rule, has his special hymn, and to these specially helpful hymns I wish to call attention.

HER MAJESTY THE QUEEN.
    Marriage hymns.
    Funeral hymns.
THE PRINCE OF WALES.
    Nearer my God, to Thee.
THE DUKE OF ARGYLL.
    O God of Bethel.
EDITOR OF " DAILY TELEGRAPH " (SIR E. ARNOLD).
    Ken's Evening Hymn.
    Longfellow's Psalm of Life.
MR. ASQUITH.
    Our God, our help in ages past.

CANON BARKER.
   One sweetly solemn thought comes to me o'er and o'er.
   I hear Thy welcome voice.
   Stand up, stand up for Jesus (lovely).
   I need Thee every hour.
   I think when I read that sweet story.
H. W. BEECHER.
   Jesu, Lover of my soul.
HEAD MASTER OF MARLBOROUGH (MR. BELL).
   Now thank we all our God. — *Winkworth*.
   In the hour of trial. — *Montgomery*.
   Come, Holy Ghost, our souls inspire. — *Cosin*.
   And now, O Father, mindful of the love. — *Bright*.
   I prais'd the earth in beauty seen. — *Heber*.
      And some 20 others.
MISS BRADDON.
   Lead, kindly light.
   Abide with me.
   Rock of ages.
   Bishop Ken's evening hymn.
JOHN BRIGHT.
   Our God, our help in ages past.
THE DUKE OF CAMBRIDGE.
   Onward, Christian soldiers.
MONCURE D. CONWAY.
   Come, O thou traveller unknown. — *Wesley*.
   Do not crouch to-day and worship the old past. — *Procter*.
   Ring out, wild bells. — *Tennyson*.
S. R. CROCKETT.
   23rd Psalm — The Lord is my Shepherd.
   142nd Psalm — I to the hills will lift mine eyes.
   103rd Psalm — O thou, my soul, bless God the Lord.
   67th Psalm.
   145th Psalm.
   O God of Bethel, by whose hand.
OLIVER CROMWELL.
   117th Psalm.
   68th Psalm — Let God arise, and let His foes be scattered.
DEAN OF CANTERBURY (F. W. FARRAR).
   Cowper, Keble, Watts, Wesley, Faber, and Montgomery have all helped me.
   I can scarcely ever join in "For ever with the Lord" without tears.
SIR H. H. FOWLER, M. P.
   Rock of ages.
   Jesu, Lover of my soul.
HARRY FURNISS.
   Psalm of Life.

# APPENDIX III.

**REV. CHARLES GARRETT, LIVERPOOL.**
Now I have found the ground whereon. — *Rothe.*
Saviour, Prince of Israel's race. — *Wesley.*
Souls of men, why will ye scatter. — *Faber.*
Come, Thou Fount of every blessing. — *R. Robinson.*
A safe stronghold our God is still. — *Luther.*
When wilt Thou save the people? — *Elliott.*

**W. LLOYD GARRISON.**
Awake, my soul, stretch every nerve.
Ye tribes of Adam far.
Rise, my soul, and stretch thy wings.

**MR. GLADSTONE** never made a list of his favourite hymns.
Lead, kindly light.
Rock of ages.

**SARAH GRAND.**
Calm me, my God, and keep me calm.
Call me, dear Saviour, I will wait Thee.

**GUSTAVUS ADOLPHUS.**
Battle hymn.

**NEWMAN HALL.**
How sweet the name of Jesus sounds.
Jesu, Lover of my soul.
Rock of ages.
Guide me, O Thou Great Jehovah.
Abide with me.

**THOMAS HARDY.**
Thou turnest man, O Lord, to dust. — *Tate* and *Brady.*
Awake, my soul, and with the sun.
Lead, kindly light. — *Newman.*

**BISHOP OF HEREFORD.**
Saviour, who hast at Thy command. — *T. Colvill.*
Jesu, where'er Thy people meet. — *W. Cowper.*
Come, let us join our friends above. — *C. Wesley.*

**SILAS D. HOCKING.**
Strong Son of God. — *Tennyson.*
The Eternal Goodness. — *Whittier.*
Abide with me. — *Lyte.*
In heavenly love abiding. — *Waring.*

**REV. H. PRICE HUGHES.**
Jesu, Lover of my soul.
A safe stronghold our God is still.
Te Deum laudamus.
Come, let us join our cheerful songs.
Come, O thou traveller unknown.

**W. JOHNSTON, M. P.**
The Lord's my Shepherd.
At even, ere the sun was set.

RICHD. LE GALLIENNE.
　Lead, kindly light.
　Peace, perfect peace.
CANON LIDDON.
　Our God, our help in ages past (one of the three best).
MRS. LYNN LINTON.
　My God, my Father.
　Nearer, my God, to Thee.
　Lead, kindly light.
SIR JOHN LUBBOCK (out of 20 or more hymns).
　New every morning is the love.
　While shepherds watched their flocks by night.
　Jesus Christ is risen to-day, Alleluia!
　The Church's one foundation.
　Hark, hark, my soul! angelic songs are swelling.
　Brief life is here our portion.
　As pants the hart for cooling streams.
　'T is gone, that bright and orbed blaze. — *Keble.*
　O Lord, my God, do Thou Thy holy will. — *Keble.*
　Why should we faint and fear to live alone. — *Keble.*
REV. D. MACRAE (Dundee).
　My God, I thank Thee. — *Procter.*
　I heard the voice of Jesus say. — *Bonar.*
　Sun of my soul. — *Keble.*
　One holy Church of God appears. — *S. W. Longfellow.*
　God bless the little children. — *Page Hopps.*
EDITOR "DAILY CHRONICLE" (H. W. MASSINGHAM) (not in order of helpfulness, but suggestions).
　Thou hidden love of God.
　My God, I love Thee not because.
　Come, O thou traveller unknown.
　Christ, whose glories fill the sky.
　Dies iræ.
JUSTIN MCCARTHY, M.P.
　Adeste fideles.
　Lead, kindly light.
MRS. ALICE MEYNELL.
　Abide with me.
　My God, my Father, while I stray.
　Sun of my soul.
　Art thou weary, art thou languid.
　Holy, holy, holy, Lord God Almighty.
　Sweet Saviour, bless us ere we go.
　Jesus lives.
　Our blest Redeemer.
PROFESSOR MAX MÜLLER.
　Caput cruentatum (strong impression as a child).
　Lead, kindly light.

# APPENDIX III.    269

Professor Max Müller — *Continued.*
   Cometh sunshine after rain.
   Father, I know that all my life.
Dr. Rigg.
   Jesu, Thy boundless love to me. — *P. Gerhardt.*
   Now I have found the ground whereon. — *Rothe*, translated by *J. Wesley.*
   Thou hidden love of God, Whose height. — *Tersteegen*, translated by *J. Wesley.*
   Come, Saviour Jesus, from above. — *Madame Bourignon.*
   Weary of wandering from my God. — *Charles Wesley.*
Lady Henry Somerset.
   The will of God. — *Faber.*
   Pilgrims. — *A. Procter.*
   My triumph. — *Whittier.*
   A first sorrow.
M. H. Spielmann (Jewish).
   Adôn 'Olam.
   Tigdal.
   Shemong.
Rev. Thomas Spurgeon.
   There is a fountain filled with blood.
The Duchess of Sutherland (who has compiled a private hymnal for use in Trentham Church).
   And now, O Father, mindful of the love.
The President of the Wesleyan Conference (Rev. D. J. Waller).
   The God of Abraham praise.
   Ere God had built the mountains.
   Thou Shepherd of Israel and mine.
   There is a wideness in God's mercy. — *Faber.*
Head Master of Harrow (Dr. Welldon).
   Hark! my soul, it is the Lord.
   Our God, our help in ages past.
   Rock of ages.
   Holy, holy, holy! Lord God Almighty.
Archdeacon Wilson, of Manchester.
   Father, whate'er of earthly bliss. — *Steele.*
   How sweet the name of Jesus sounds. —*Doddridge.*
   Come, ye that love the Lord. — *Watts.*
   O Thou to whose all-searching sight. — *J. Wesley.*
   When all Thy mercies, O my God. — *Addison.*
   Jesus, whene'er Thy people meet. — *Cowper.*
   Glorious things of Thee are spoken. — *Newton.*
   Thou hidden love of God. — *Tersteegen* and *Wesley.*
   Ken's and Keble's morning and evening hymns.
   There is a land of pure delight. — *Watts.*
   Who follow Christ whate'er betide. — *C. Winkworth.*

**Archdeacon Wilson of Manchester** — *Continued.*
    Who shall ascend to the Holy Place. — *Hankinson.*
    O love divine, how sweet thou art. — *C. Wesley.*
    Be Thou my guardian and my guide. — *J. Williams.*
    My God, and is Thy table spread. — *Doddridge.*

**Charles Wesley.**
    O for a thousand tongues to sing.

**Bishop Moorhouse** (attaches the deepest and most sacred associations and memories of good).
    Jesu, Lover of my soul.
    My God, my Father, while I stray.
    Sun of my soul, Thou Saviour dear.
    Our God, our help in ages past.
    O God of Bethel, by whose hand.

**Sir Evelyn Wood.**
    Lead, kindly light.
    Fierce raged the tempest.
    And now, Father, mindful of the love.
    Eternal Father! strong to save.

**John Wesley.**
    Depth of mercy, can there be.

# INDEX OF FIRST LINES.

|  | PAGE |
|---|---|
| A charge to keep I have | 215 |
| A few more years shall roll | 241 |
| A sure stronghold our God is He | 53 |
| Abide with me, fast falls the eventide | 207 |
| Adeste fideles | 80 |
| All hail the power of Jesu's name | 29 |
| All people that on earth do dwell | 30 |
| Allons, enfants de la Patrie | 49 |
| "Almost persuaded:" now to believe | 177 |
| Angels holy | 37 |
| Art thou weary, art thou languid | 74 |
| At even, ere the sun was set | 209 |
| At the cross her station keeping | 86 |
| Ave, Maria, gratia plena | 236 |
| Ave, maris stella | 237 |
| Awake, my soul, and with the sun | 202 |
| Begone, unbelief | 119 |
| Blessed Lord, in Thee is refuge | 142 |
| Brief life is here our portion | 253 |
| By Christ redeemed, in Christ restored | 240 |
| Christ, the Lord, is risen to-day | 90 |
| "Christian! seek not yet repose" | 170 |
| Come, Holy Ghost, our souls inspire | 77 |
| Come, let us join our friends above | 244 |
| Come, O Thou traveller unknown | 154 |
| Come, Thou fount of every blessing | 196 |
| Come, ye sinners, poor and wretched | 179 |
| Courage, brother! do not stumble | 220 |
| Curb for the stubborn steed | 72 |
| Day of wrath! O day of mourning | 96 |
| De profundis clamavi ad te, Domine | 94 |
| Dies iræ, dies illa | 98 |
| Ein' feste Burg ist unser Gott | 54 |
| Eternal Father, strong to save | 239 |
| Faith of our fathers! living still | 238 |
| Father, I know that all my life | 126 |
| Father of All! in ev'ry Age | 224 |
| Fear not, O little flock, the foe | 58 |
| For thee, O dear, dear country | 255 |
| Forward! be our watchword | 171 |
| From Greenland's icy mountains | 173 |
| Give me the wings of faith to rise | 245 |

# INDEX OF FIRST LINES.

|  | PAGE |
|---|---|
| Give to the winds thy fears | 124 |
| Gloria in excelsis | 69 |
| Glory be to God on high | 68 |
| Glory to Thee, my God, this night | 213 |
| God bless our native land | 44 |
| God moves in a mysterious way | 116 |
| God save our gracious Queen | 39 |
| Gracious Spirit, Holy Ghost | 150 |
| Guide me, O Thou Great Jehovah | 110 |
| Hail, bright Star of ocean | 236 |
| Hail, gladdening Light, of His pure glory pour'd | 70 |
| Hail, Mary, full of grace | 236 |
| Hark, my soul! it is the Lord | 145 |
| Hark! the herald angels sing | 81 |
| Have mercy upon me, O God | 82 |
| He leadeth me! Oh, blessèd thought | 114 |
| Hear what the voice from heaven proclaims | 246 |
| Holy, holy, holy, Lord God Almighty | 33 |
| How blest the righteous when he dies | 247 |
| How sweet the name of Jesus sounds | 187 |
| I do not ask, O Lord, that life may be | 114 |
| I heard the voice of Jesus say | 192 |
| I lay me down to sleep | 250 |
| I live for those who love me | 231 |
| I need Thee every hour, most gracious Lord | 196 |
| I to the hills will lift mine eyes | 129 |
| If the Lord me sorrow send | 138 |
| Immortal Love, for ever full | 226 |
| In some way or other the Lord will provide | 118 |
| In the Cross of Christ I glory | 200 |
| In the waves and mighty waters | 257 |
| Jerusalem, my happy home | 251 |
| Jerusalem the golden | 256 |
| Jesu dulcis memoria | 187 |
| Jesu! Lover of my soul | 151 |
| Jesus, and shall it ever be? | 199 |
| Jesus shall reign where'er the sun | 175 |
| Jesus, still lead on | 113 |
| Jesus, the very thought of Thee | 186 |
| Just as I am, without one plea | 144 |
| Lead, kindly Light, amid the encircling gloom | 107 |
| Let God arise, and scattered let all his en'mies be | 61 |
| Let us, with a gladsome mind | 34 |
| Life! we've been long together | 247 |
| Lo! He comes with clouds descending | 100 |
| Lord, it belongs not to my care | 130 |
| Lord, now lettest Thou Thy servant depart in peace | 69 |
| Lord of all being, throned afar | 229 |
| Love divine, all loves excelling | 188 |

# INDEX OF FIRST LINES.

|  | PAGE |
|---|---|
| Magnificat | 67 |
| Mine eyes have seen the glory of the coming of the Lord | 59 |
| Miserere mei, Deus | 84 |
| Must Jesus bear the Cross alone | 199 |
| My country! 'tis of thee | 46 |
| My God, I love Thee; not because | 156 |
| My God, my Father, blissful name | 135 |
| My God, my Father, while I stray | 134 |
| My soul doth magnify the Lord | 66 |
| Nearer, my God, to Thee | 159 |
| Now I have found the ground wherein | 185 |
| Now thank we all our God | 31 |
| Now the labourer's task is o'er | 249 |
| Nunc dimittis | 70 |
| O come, all ye faithful | 79 |
| O Deus, ego amo Te | 157 |
| O for a closer walk with God | 164 |
| O for a heart to praise my God | 162 |
| O give ye praise unto the Lord | 62 |
| O God of Bethel, by whose hand | 182 |
| O God of Truth, whose living word | 163 |
| O Jesu, King most wonderful | 194 |
| O Jesus, I have promised | 165 |
| O Lord, how happy should we be | 132 |
| O Love, that wilt not let me go | 146 |
| O Sacred Head once wounded | 197 |
| O Thou, from whom all goodness flows | 136 |
| O timely happy, timely wise | 205 |
| Oft in sorrow, oft in woe | 169 |
| Oh for a thousand tongues to sing | 190 |
| Oh to be nothing, nothing | 167 |
| Onward, Christian soldiers! marching as to war | 168 |
| Our Blest Redeemer, ere He breathed | 153 |
| Our Friend, our Brother, and our Lord | 227 |
| Our God, our help in ages past | 181 |
| Out of the depths have I cried unto Thee, O Lord | 94 |
| Pange lingua gloriosi | 92 |
| Peace, perfect peace | 201 |
| Praise God from Whom all blessings flow | 33 |
| Rescue the perishing, care for the dying | 222 |
| Rock of Ages, cleft for me | 139 |
| Safe in the arms of Jesus | 193 |
| Saviour, again to Thy dear name we raise | 210 |
| Saviour, breathe an evening blessing | 212 |
| Saviour, when in dust to Thee | 102 |
| Si scopron le tombe, si levano i morti | 64 |
| Sing, my tongue, the Saviour's glory | 91 |
| Sleep on, belovèd, sleep, and take thy rest | 248 |
| So here hath been dawning | 204 |

# INDEX OF FIRST LINES.

| | PAGE |
|---|---|
| Soldiers of Christ, arise | 170 |
| Souls of men! why will ye scatter | 230 |
| Sowing the seed by the dawn-light fair | 223 |
| Stabat Mater dolorosa | 88 |
| Standing by a purpose true | 221 |
| Sun of my soul, Thou Saviour dear | 206 |
| Sweet Saviour, bless us ere we go | 211 |
| Take my life, and let it be | 161 |
| Te Deum laudamus | 26 |
| Tell me not, in mournful numbers | 215 |
| That day of wrath, that dreadful day | 95 |
| The Lord's my shepherd, I'll not want | 110 |
| The spacious firmament on high | 232 |
| The Universal Master reigned | 234 |
| There is a fountain filled with blood | 148 |
| There is a land of pure delight | 252 |
| There were ninety and nine | 176 |
| Thou hidden Love of God, whose height | 191 |
| Thy way, not mine, O Lord | 132 |
| Time is earnest, passing by | 178 |
| 'T is my happiness below | 133 |
| Uplifted the tombstones | 65 |
| Veni, Creator | 78 |
| We plough the fields and scatter | 242 |
| We praise Thee, O God | 24 |
| When all Thy mercies, O my God | 36 |
| When gathering clouds around I view | 117 |
| When I survey the wondrous Cross | 147 |
| When our heads are bowed with woe | 101 |
| When the weary, seeking rest | 104 |
| When wilt Thou save the people? | 45 |
| Without haste and without rest | 217 |
| Work, for the night is coming | 219 |
| Workman of God, O lose not heart | 218 |
| Ye sons of France, awake to glory | 51 |
| Yn y dyfroedd mawr a'r tonau | 257 |

## INDEX OF AUTHORS.

| | |
|---|---|
| Adams, Mrs. | 159 |
| Addison, Joseph | 36, 232 |
| Alexander, Dr. (Translator) | 197 |
| Alford, Dean | 171 |
| Alstyne, Mrs. Van | 193 |
| Altenburg, Pastor | 58 |
| Anonymous | 24, 39, 79, 118, 167, 177, 178, 199, 215, 222, 223, 236, 238, 250, 257 |

# INDEX OF AUTHORS.

| | PAGE |
|---|---|
| Anstice, Rev. Prof. | 132 |
| Aquinas, Thomas | 91 |
| Auber, Harriet | 153 |
| Banks, G. Linnæus | 231 |
| Barbauld, Mrs. | 247 |
| Baring-Gould, Rev. S. | 168 |
| Baxter, Richard | 130 |
| Bernard of Clairvaux | 186, 194, 197 |
| Bernard of Cluny | 253, 255, 256 |
| Bickersteth, Bishop | 201 |
| Blackie, Prof. J. S. | 37 |
| Bliss, Philip | 221 |
| Bode, Rev. J. E. | 165 |
| Bonar, Horatius | 104, 132, 192, 241 |
| Booth, Herbert | 142 |
| Bowring, Sir John | 200 |
| Campbell, Miss T. M. (Translator) | 242 |
| Carlyle, Thomas | 204 |
| Carlyle, Thomas (Translator) | 53 |
| Caswall, E. (Translator) | 156 |
| Cennick, John, and Charles Wesley | 100 |
| Claudius, Matthias | 242 |
| Clephane, Elizabeth C. | 176 |
| Cohen, Rev. F. L. (Translator) | 234 |
| Cosin, Bishop (Translator) | 77 |
| Cowper, William | 116, 133, 145, 148, 164 |
| Doddridge, Dr. | 182 |
| Doudney, Miss Sarah | 248 |
| Edmeston, Dr. | 212 |
| Ellerton, Rev. John | 210, 249 |
| Elliott, Charlotte | 134, 144, 170 |
| Elliott, Ebenezer | 45 |
| F. B. P. | 251 |
| Faber, F. W. | 211, 218, 230 |
| Gerhardt, Paulus | 124 |
| Gilmore, Joseph H. | 114 |
| Goethe | 217 |
| Grant, Sir Robert | 102, 117 |
| Gregg, Joseph | 199 |
| Hart, Joseph | 179 |
| Havergal, Miss F. R. | 161 |
| Haweis, Thomas | 136 |
| Hawks, Mrs. A. S. | 196 |
| Heber, Bishop | 33, 173 |
| Holmes, O. W. | 229 |
| Howe, Julia Ward | 59 |
| Hughes, Tom | 163 |
| Irons, Dr. (Translator) | 96 |
| Jacopone | 86 |

## INDEX OF AUTHORS.

|  | PAGE |
|---|---|
| Keble, John | 205, 206 |
| Keble, John (Translator) | 70 |
| Ken, Bishop | 32, 202, 213 |
| Kethe, W. | 30 |
| Longfellow, Henry W. | 215 |
| Luther, Martin | 53 |
| Lyte, Rev. H. F. | 207 |
| Macleod, Dr. Norman | 220 |
| Matheson, Dr. | 146 |
| Mercantini, L. | 64 |
| Milman, Dean | 101 |
| Milton, John | 34 |
| Neale, Dr. (Translator) | 74 |
| Newman, Cardinal | 107 |
| Newton, John | 119, 187 |
| Perronet, E. | 29 |
| Plumptre, Dean | 72 |
| Pope, Alexander | 224 |
| Procter, Adelaide | 114 |
| Rawson, George | 240 |
| Rinkart, Martin | 31 |
| Robinson, Robert | 196 |
| Rothe, Johann Andreas | 185 |
| Rouget de Lille | 49 |
| Sankey, Ira D. | 219 |
| Scott, Sir Walter (Translator) | 95 |
| Smith, Samuel Francis | 46 |
| Steele, Anne | 135 |
| Stephen the Sabaite | 74 |
| Tersteegen, Gerhard | 191 |
| Toplady, Rev. A. M. | 139 |
| Twells, H. | 209 |
| Waring, Miss | 126 |
| Watts, Dr. Isaac | 147, 175, 181, 245, 246, 252 |
| Wesley, Charles | 81, 90, 151, 154, 162, 170, 188, 190, 244 |
| Wesley, Charles, and John Cennick | 100 |
| Wesley, John (Translator) | 124, 185, 191 |
| White, Henry Kirke | 169 |
| Whiting, William | 239 |
| Whittier, J. G. | 226, 227 |
| Williams, William | 110 |
| Willich, Ernst von | 138 |
| Winkworth, Catherine (Translator) | 31 |
| Wordsworth, Bishop | 150 |
| Xavier, Francis | 156 |
| Zinzendorf, Count | 113 |

www.ingramcontent.com/pod-product-compliance
Lightning Source LLC
Chambersburg PA
CBHW031944230426
43672CB00010B/2039